Beyond Suffering & Enlightenment

PM Deviprasadh

Contents

Preface

Why I Compiled a Book on Buddhism, and Why You Should (Probably) bother to Read It

Let's be honest—do we really need another book about Buddhism? After all, the world isn't exactly short on books. Hasn't everyone already read a dozen or so books on the Buddha and achieved inner peace by lunchtime? (Okay, maybe not.)

So, why this book? Well, it's my attempt to unravel the mysteries and miseries of existence—and to figure out why my happiness seems to vanish the moment I open my eyes each morning. (Okay, maybe the happiness thing is a deeper mystery best left to the professional philosophers.) What I *have* tried to tackle, however, is the fascinating, sometimes perplexing world of Buddhist thought and practice as a potential path out of human suffering.

Now, you might be wondering: what qualifies me to write a book on Buddhism? The short answer is: *absolutely nothing.*

Nada. Zilch. Zero. I'm not a monk. I'm just an ordinary person with a healthy dose of curiosity, a slightly unhealthy caffeine addiction, and absolutely zero formal qualifications to write about Buddhism. But hey, who needs qualifications when you have enthusiasm? I've done my research *(quite painfully, i might add)*, and I'm ready to share what I've learned. Labels like "layman" or "enlightened monk" are irrelevant here. After all, suffering doesn't discriminate.

Existence is suffering—a truth that led me to explore religious texts and philosophy. For me, Buddhism just made sense. Nothing else quite did. Is this book my original work? Not at all. Every truth I've shared has already been voiced by someone before me. I've simply compiled stories and teachings passed down by Buddhist masters over centuries. After all, no one can claim exclusive ownership of universal truths.

Studying Buddhism can be challenging. The Buddha's life story and teachings aren't always presented as a clear, cohesive picture. Ancient texts, like the Pali Canon—the foundation of this book and the only complete surviving collection of early Buddhist scriptures used by Theravada Buddhists in Sri Lanka and Southeast Asia—don't provide a straightforward timeline or a simple explanation of his ideas.

This book isn't meant to be the definitive guide to Buddhism. If you're looking for high-level academic discussions or debates about translations of ancient texts, you'll want to find a book written by someone who *actually knows* their heads from their tails. Instead, this book is more of a friendly exploratory journey with someone who's also trying to figure things out.

Who was Siddhartha, the man who became the Buddha? What can his teachings offer us? Can I, too, embark on the path to enlightenment? What does that path even look like?

As the Buddha said, ***"One stills and clears the mind and then turns it towards investigation and insight."***

Just remember—if you suddenly achieve enlightenment halfway through the book, don't thank me. And if you figure out the happiness thing, for the love of all Buddhas, please let me know.

Chapter 1

The legend of Buddhas before Siddhartha

Buddhist tradition teaches that every living thing experiences a never-ending cycle of birth, death, and rebirth. Before becoming a Buddha (someone who has reached complete wisdom), a person lives many lives in different forms - as humans, animals, or divine beings. Before their final life as a Buddha, they spend time in a heaven called Tushita (meaning - "a place of happiness"). Here, they are known as a bodhisattva - someone on the path to becoming enlightened. They stay in this heaven until the perfect time comes for them to be born as a human and become a Buddha. This heavenly stay is just the first step in their spiritual journey, which they achieve by practicing good qualities Paramithas) / perfections across many lives.

Long ago, there was a holy man named Sumedha (also called Megha) who met a previous Buddha named Dīpaṃkara. This meeting changed Sumedha's life - he was so inspired by Dīpaṃkara's wisdom and compassion that he decided to become a Buddha himself. To achieve this goal, Sumedha worked on developing ten good qualities: generosity, good behavior, letting go of desires, hard work, wisdom, patience, truthfulness, determination, kindness, and staying calm in all situations.

By developing these qualities, Sumedha became a bodhisattva - someone who is on the path to becoming a Buddha. Eventually, he was reborn as Gautama Buddha in the 5th century BCE. There are many stories about the Buddha's previous lives, called jātakas. These stories show how he developed these good qualities over many lifetimes. These stories are very important in Buddhist culture. We wont go into those now. Our story focusses on Siddhartha Gautama. While it's special when a Buddha appears in the world, it's not a one-time event.

A new Buddha appears when people have forgotten the teachings of previous Buddhas and when they're ready to learn these teachings again.

Chapter 2
Early life of Siddhartha

In sixth century BCE Northern India, the land was divided into monarchical states (Janapadas) and non-monarchical states (Sanghs or Ganas). The Sakyas of Kapilvatsu were one such non-monarchical state, governed by rotating ruling families with a King. Siddharth Gautama's father Suddhodana was the king at the time of his birth. Though initially an independent kingdom, the Sakyas later came under Kosala kingdom's influence. King Suddhodana married Queen Mahamaya and later her sister Mahaprajapati. As a wealthy King with vast influence, he lived a life of luxury. Siddharth Gautama was born during an auspicious midsummer festival in the month of Ashad. His mother Mahamaya participated in the seven-day celebration with devotion, enjoying the festivities & prayed for a child. On the final day, after giving alms and taking her vows, Mahamaya had a significant dream.

In it, four world-guardians took her to the Himalayas where she was prepared to meet a divine being. The Bodhisatta

Sumedha appeared and asked her to be his mother in his final earthly birth.

When Mahamaya shared this dream with her husband Suddhodana, he consulted eight Brahmin diviners for its meaning. The eight wise men said, "Don't worry. You will have a son who will become one of two things: either a great king if he stays at home, or if he leaves home to become a spiritual teacher, he will become the Buddha - The one who helps others understand the truth about life."

Following the customs of ancient India, Mahamaya decided to have her baby at her parents' home. On her way there, she stopped to rest in a beautiful Lumbini grove garden. The garden was full of flowers and fruits, with bees buzzing and birds singing. While resting there, she gave birth to her son in 563 BCE on the full moon day of Vaishakha. Everyone celebrated the birth of the prince with great festivities.

A wise man named Asita lived in the Himalayas. On the day of Siddhartha's birth, he saw something amazing - gods were celebrating in the sky and shouting "Buddha!". Using his spiritual wisdom, he learned they were celebrating because a very special baby had just been born to King Suddhodana.

Asita traveled to the palace with his nephew Nardatta to see this special baby. When Asita met the king, he blessed him & said he wanted to see the newborn prince. The king told Asita that the baby was sleeping, but Asita said that divine babies like this one don't sleep for long. Just as he expected, the baby woke up soon and was brought to meet him. Asita carefully looked at the baby and found thirty-two special marks on his body that showed his greatness. According to ancient wisdom, a person with these marks would become either a great ruler or a fully enlightened teacher called a Buddha. Asita was sure this child would choose to become a Buddha.

When Asita saw the baby, he bowed down in respect and said, "This is a wonderful being who has come into the world." But then, surprisingly, he began to cry. Suddhodhana was worried and asked if this meant something bad would happen to his son.

Asita explained, "No, no - These are tears of Joy! I'm crying because I'm very old and won't live long enough to see this child become the world's teacher he's meant to be."

Asita continued, "This boy will become a Buddha - an enlightened being. He'll teach wisdom in a new way that will help many people find happiness. His teachings will be perfect from start to finish, clear and pure. Just like the rare Oudumbara flower that blooms only once in a very long time, Buddhas are very rare in this world. Your son will help countless people find their way out of suffering. But I'm sad because I won't live to see it happen."

The baby was named Siddharth Gautama, which means "he whose purpose is accomplished." Sadly, just five days after his naming ceremony, his mother Mahamaya became very sick. Before she died, she spoke to her husband Suddhodana and her sister Prajapati. She told them she believed what Asita had said about her son's future, and she asked Prajapati to take care of her baby. Then she peacefully accepted her death, leaving little Siddharth without a mother when he was only seven days old.

Education & Marriage

Siddharth started his formal education at age eight. His teachers were the same eight wise men who had interpreted his mother's dream before his birth. He learned philosophy from a teacher named Sabbamittain and meditation from Bhardawaj in his hometown of Kapilavatsu.

From an early age, Siddharth showed great kindness that set him apart from others. Unlike other warrior princes who didn't question the poor treatment of workers, Siddharth spoke up against it. He chose to join farmers in their harvest festival and refused to go hunting, even though hunting was expected of young warrior princes like him. His stepmother Prajapati Gautami told him that as someone born into the warrior class (Kshatriya), he had to learn fighting and hunting. But Siddharth disagreed with these old traditions. He believed that understanding each other through compassion was better than using violence. He tried to teach his friends how to focus, have compassion & meditate, hoping they would learn to wish happiness for everyone. But his friends were more interested in everyday sensual pleasures and hunting activities. His parents didn't like that he practiced meditation. They thought it wasn't right for someone who was supposed to become a warrior prince.

Siddharth taught a simple but powerful idea about meditation: "Meditation helps us love all living things equally. Usually, we put things in different categories - we call some people friends and others enemies, we treat pets one way and wild animals another way, we love some and hate others. But meditation helps us see past these differences and treat everyone with kindness."

One story clearly shows young Siddharth's compassion. He once found a bird that his cousin Devadatta had shot and wounded. Siddharth took care of the bird until it got better. When Devadatta said the bird belonged to him because he shot it, Siddharth argued that the person who cares for a living being has more right to it than the person who hurts it. Even though this made his cousin angry, Siddharth stood by what he believed was right.

Siddhartha sought out to visit hermits and monks to learn more despite his father's disapproval. Unlike the power-seeking warriors and priests, these monks renounced worldly possessions to pursue spiritual liberation through their study of the Vedas and Upanishads. Many such hermits lived in the neighboring kingdoms of Kosala and Magadha, which Siddhartha longed to visit.

King Suddhodana feared his son might become a monk as predicted. He confided in his brother Dronodanaraja about his worry that Siddhartha would abandon his royal responsibilities. Dronodanaraja proposed a solution: arrange Siddhartha's marriage to a princess to divert his attention from spiritual matters.

The king agreed and tasked queen Gotami with arranging a marriage. She organized social gatherings where Siddhartha could meet young people. These events led to a martial arts competition at Kunau Lake, drawing participants from the kingdoms of Sakya and Koliya.

Yasodhara, daughter of King Dandapani and Queen Pamita of the Koliya kingdom, served as hostess at the competition. Siddhartha dominated all events—archery, swordsmanship, horse racing, and weightlifting. Yasodhara presented him with a white elephant as his prize, offering graceful congratulations.

One day, Siddhartha came upon Princess Yasodhara in a poor village, where she was tending to sick children with her maid. Despite her royal status, she was dressed in plainclothes, she treated their ailments and washed their clothes. "I've been doing this for almost two years," she told Siddhartha when he asked. Their conversation revealed that Yasodhara also shared his questioning of traditions and social inequities. Like him, she felt uncomfortable with royal privilege and court politics. Unable to create large-scale change as a woman, she had chosen to help others through charitable work.

Siddhartha found himself increasingly drawn to Princess Yasodhara. Among all the young women he had met, she alone combined beauty with a spirit that matched his own. When he proposed marriage, she accepted.Siddhartha and Yasodhara were married that autumn in a joyous celebration. A year later they had a son, **Rahula.**

Siddharth's father, King Suddhodana, was happy about the marriage. But he was still worried about the old prophecy made by sage Asita. To prevent Siddharth from becoming a monk, the king tried to keep his son interested in life's pleasures. He built three beautiful palaces - one for each season. Each palace had beautiful gardens and everything someone could want for a comfortable life. The king asked his minister Udayin to bring attractive female dancers to entertain Siddharth. But Siddharth wasn't interested - he only saw how everything in life was temporary.

The minister

Udayin then tried talking to Siddharth privately, telling him that a prince like him should enjoy life's pleasures like other great men had done before him. Siddhartha responded firmly to Udayin's persuasive words: "Though I understand worldly pleasures, I cannot find joy in what is temporary. Even if women's beauty were eternal, pursuing desires would still be unworthy of wisdom. Do not point to great men who fell to desire - they met their destruction through it. True greatness lies not in greedily craving earthly attachments or lack of self-control. I reject deception, in any form. Without truth and genuine connection, compliance with sensual desires is meaningless."

Troubled by his son's disinterest in worldly life, Suddhodana and his ministers tried multiple times to change Siddharth's mind but were unsuccessful.

Chapter 3

Inititiation into the Sakhya Sangh & parivraja

When Siddharth Gautama was twenty years old, he joined the Sakya Sangh, which was the local community council in Kapilavatsu. The council leader Senapati nominated him, and after three voting rounds where no one opposed Siddharth, he became a member. When Senapati asked him questions about his duties to the Sangh, Siddharth humbly said he was honored to be included in the Sangh but didn't yet know what his duties would be.

"It's quite simple," he explained. "You must protect only the interests of the Sakya people at all costs, come to all meetings, report any bad behavior honestly, and deal with any accusations fairly."

"If you commit rape, murder, theft, or lie under oath, you'll lose your membership," he added. "I understand and will follow these rules," Siddharth answered.

After eight years as an exemplary member of the Sakya Sangh, Siddharth faced a crisis. A conflict arose between the Sakyas and their neighboring kingdom, the Koliyas, over the waters of the River Rohini that divided their lands. The kingdoms shared the river for irrigation, but frequent water disputes led to violence between their workers. After minor skirmishes injuries occurred on both sides, war seemed inevitable. The Senapati convened the Sakya Sangh and moved to declare war. "The Koliyas' aggression must be answered," he said. "I propose war. Any opposed may speak."

Siddharth Gautama rose and opposed the resolution: "War solves nothing and only breeds more conflict. The slayer invites slaying, and the conqueror invites conquest. Let's not jump into war, First, we should find out who's really responsible. I've heard that our own people were also attacking the Koliyas."

The Senapati admitted, "Yes, our men did attack, but we had the right to use the water at that time."

Siddharth said, "So we're also responsible for this problem. Here's my suggestion: let each side choose two people, and those four can pick a fifth person together. This group can then work out a fair solution peacefully." Most people voted against Siddharth's peaceful suggestion.

Siddharth tried again to stop it: "The Sakyas and Koliyas are related to each other. We shouldn't fight and destroy our own family."

The Senapati disagreed, saying that according to their ancient laws, warriors must fight even against their brothers to protect their kingdom. He talked about how different social groups had different duties to follow. He said "According to the

Chaturvana system, Kshatriyas (The warriors) must fight to protect their kingdom's interests at all costs."

Siddharth replied simply: "True Dharma teaches us that hate cannot stop hate, it becomes a never ending cycle of suffering - only love can do that." But the Senapati stopped him from saying more and wanted all Sakya men aged 20 to 50 to join the army and fight against the Koliyas. Though some disagreed with the decision, they were too afraid to speak against the powerful senapati & remained quiet.

Siddharth was the only one brave enough to speak up. "I cannot support this barbaric action over a petty water dispute, when peaceful solutions are still possible" he said. "I refuse to fight in this war."

The Senapati reminded Siddhartha what a strong and fine warrior prince he was, and that Siddhartha had sworn to follow the Sankhya Sangh's decisions. He emphasized Siddhartha's princely duty to fight and impose military superiority over the Koliyas. The Senapati warned about the public shame that would befall him and his kingdom if the Koliyas were not taught a lesson. But Siddhartha replied that doing what was right for his people mattered more than avoiding shame. He also cautioned that this war would only create an opportunity for their other enemies to seize their kingdom.

This enraged the Senapati. He threatened to punish Siddhartha's family by cutting them off from society and seizing their lands—actions he could take without the king's approval. He gave Siddhartha an ultimatum: either join the war against the Koliyas, or renounce his title as prince, forfeit his Kshatriya class status, and leave the kingdom to become

Parivrajaka (wandering spiritual monks) who were exempt from warfare.

"Don't punish my family," Siddhartha told everyone. "They've done nothing wrong. If you want to punish someone, punish me—either send me to prison for forfeiting my duties or sentence me to death. I won't ask my father, the king, to help me." The Senapati had the authority to punish anyone who did not comply with the duties prescribed to their societal class. However, he worried that killing or imprisoning Siddhartha would enrage the king. When he expressed this delicate position to Siddhartha in private, Siddhartha offered to become a Parivrajaka. Though uncertain of his family's approval, he promised the Sangh he would leave with or without their permission.

At the end of the meeting, a cunning young member suggested they wait to start the war until after Siddhartha had fully undertaken Parivraja, ensuring the king wouldn't implicate the Sakya Sangh. Everyone agreed to this plan. When the meeting ended, those who had secretly opposed the war but had been too afraid to speak up felt relieved that Siddhartha had at least temporarily prevented the war by choosing to become a Parivrajaka. News of the prince's decision to become a monk reached his family before he arrived home.

When Siddhartha returned, he found his parents in tears. They begged him to stay, suggesting the whole family could leave together instead. But Siddhartha explained that he had chosen to become a Parivrajaka to protect their kingdom and honor his word to the council.

"How can you survive alone in the wild?" his mother Gautami asked. Siddharth reminded her that she came from a warrior family, and asked if she would be this sad if he died fighting in battle. She said this was different, but Siddharth explained he couldn't take everyone with him, especially since they had to care for young baby Rahula.

His father tried to convince him to wait, since the war had been delayed, unaware that the war was postponed only because Siddhartha had agreed to leave the kingdom. But Siddhartha refused: "I gave my word, which helped stop the war for now. If I break that promise, it could cause serious problems. Mother, please bless my decision—it's the right thing to do." His parents could say nothing more.

When Siddhartha went to see his wife Yashodhara, he didn't know what to say. She spoke first, telling him she knew about the council meeting. Unlike his parents, her strong and calm response pleasantly surprised him. "My lord, my love for you knows no bounds and you mean the entire world to me. Though your departure will plunge me into rivers of sorrow, I understand why you made this choice and I support you in all your decisions wholeheartedly—it's the right thing to do. I would go with you if I didn't have to care for Rahula," she said. "Stay strong. I'll look after your parents and our son. I hope your new path helps make the world better. Only promise to visit us whenever you have found what you seek." Her noble response touched Siddhartha deeply, reminding him what an extraordinary wife she was. After taking one last look at his son Rahula, he left.

Siddharth traveled to Bharadwaja's Ashram in Kapila-vatsu, accompanied by his servant Channa. When they arrived, many people gathered to see their Crown Prince undertake parivraja at such a young age. He was surprised to find his parents,

Suddhodana and Prajapati Gautami, already waiting there. He had wanted to avoid causing them pain, as saying goodbye while they shed tears and embraced him would be unbearable. Following religious custom, Siddharth gave his fancy royal clothes and jewelry to Channa. He shaved his head and put on the plain robes of a monk, which his cousin Mahanama had brought. Bharadwaja then performed a ceremony that officially made Siddharth a parivrajaka.

Remembering his promise to the Sakya council, Siddharth started his journey away from his kingdom to the Anoma river right away. When people tried to follow him, he stopped and spoke to them: "My brothers and sisters, please go back home. Even though I couldn't solve our fight with the Koliyas, you can still help create peace by talking to others about it." After hearing this, the crowd went home, and his parents returned to the palace in tears. His mother Gautami was so upset that she fainted & his old royal clothes fell into a pool of lotus flowers.

At twenty-nine, Siddharth Gautama chose renunciation (Parivraja). People marveled at this noble youth who, born to wealth and privilege, chose to fight for peace rather than war. When outvoted by his kinsmen, he accepted exile - trading riches for poverty and comfort for homelessness. His sacrifice was unprecedented, earning him the titles **"SakyaMuni"** and **"Sakya Sinha".**

Farewell to Channa the servant & Kanthaka the horse

Channa insisted on accompanying the Prince and Kanthaka to the river Anoma, and Gautama agreed. When they reached the riverbank, Gautama turned to Channa with gratitude for his loyalty and devotion. "Though I cannot reward you, your selfless love sets you apart," he said. "Take the horse and return. Tell the king I leave not from anger or desire for heaven, but from duty. Ask him not to mourn - all unions must end, all separations are inevitable. Though one may have many heirs to wealth, heirs to merit & virtue are rare. The king needs care now, and though he may say I leave at the wrong time, my duty knows no wrong time.Please tell my father not to think about me anymore, and let my mother know I don't deserve her wonderful love."

Channa bowed with his hands together and spoke sadly: "My lord, it hurts to see you go. Why would you leave the comfort of the palace to face the hardships of living in the forest? Your family - your father, mother, wife, and little son - all need you. Please let me come with you," he said earnestly, "I can't bear to go back alone and tell them you've left forever. They would never accept that you're unworthy. Please come back home with me."

Siddhartha Gautama replied gently: "Do not grieve over our parting. All beings must separate—just as birds leave their nests and clouds disperse. Even if I stayed, death would part us eventually. Nothing in this world of unions and partings truly belongs to us. Go now, dear friend, and tell Kapilavastu to release their love for me and accept my resolve." Kanthaka, Siddhartha's loyal horse, showed his sadness by licking his master's feet before he left. After saying a final goodbye, Channa bowed respectfully and Siddhartha walked away. The journey back home was somber. Channa and Kanthaka moved slowly, both consumed with grief. The horse was so distraught that he refused to eat or drink, and kept calling out for his master.

When they returned to Kapilavastu without Siddhartha, everyone was heartbroken. The people held out hope that Channa, Siddhartha's most loyal assistant, might be able to convince him to return. The citizens wept at the sight of the royal horse without its princely rider. The royal family was especially devastated—Queen Gautami fainted, his wife Yashodhara collapsed crying beside their baby, and his father King Suddhodana went to the temple to pray for his son's return.

Chapter 4

Discourse with King Bimbisara

Siddhartha Gautama traveled from the Anoma River to Rajagriha, the capital city of Magadha, renowned for its scholars and teachers. He crossed the Ganges River, rested at three holy places, and finally reached the city. People were amazed by his appearance as a humble monk and treated him with great respect. After walking 400 miles from his hometown of Kapilavastu, he made a simple shelter from leaves at the bottom of Pandava Hill, one of five hills surrounding Magadha.

The next day, while seeking food donations, crowds gathered to see him. A royal official noticed him and recalled a prediction that this man would either become enlightened or rule as a great emperor. The official told King Bimbisara about him and described how gracefully Gautama collected his food and ate alone on the hillside. Impressed, King Bimbisara went to meet him.

Finding Gautama, the king offered him half of his kingdom. The king believed someone as noble as Gautama should be a ruler rather than a monk. "Religious pursuits are for the elderly, while youth is for pleasure and middle age for wealth. Since youth's pleasures are fleeting, seize them while you can. The old naturally turn to reflection and spiritual matters. Embrace the pleasures of youth while you can, or if you seek spirituality, follow the traditional path. Many royal sages found enlightenment through ritual and sacrifice, not through renunciation."

Gautama answered the king calmly and kindly: "King, I understand why you speak this way. You come from a noble family and want to help someone you see as a friend. Bad people abandon family friendships, but good people build on their ancestors' relationships by showing kindness to each other. I deeply value true friends—those who stay loyal during hard times. After all, it's easy to be friends when things are going well. Real wealth comes from using what you have to help friends and support spiritual growth. This kind of wealth leaves no regrets when it's gone. I know your offer comes from genuine friendship and generosity. I respond with the same friendship, but I must decline."

"I'm actually afraid of worldly pleasures—more afraid than I am of snakes, lightning, or raging fires. These pleasures steal our peace of mind and our wealth. They're like mirages—they trick our minds even before we have them, and even more once they take hold of us.

"People who chase after pleasures never find true happiness, not even in heaven. They're like a fire that burns hotter with more fuel—they're never satisfied. Nothing brings more misery than the pursuit of pleasure. People only chase it because they're confused about what really matters. Once you understand how harmful it is, why would any wise person choose to pursue it?

"Even kings who rule vast lands always want more territory. People's desire for pleasure is like a bottomless ocean—it can never be filled. History shows us this truth. Take King Mandhatri—even after receiving great wealth from heaven, conquering many lands, and gaining immense power, he still wanted more. Another example is King Narahasura—he became so powerful that he ruled over the gods themselves, yet his pride and greed made him force holy men to carry him around like servants. Still, he wasn't satisfied.

"Why would anyone chase after pleasures that are actually our enemies in disguise? Even holy men who lived simply, wearing old clothes and eating only basic food, sometimes fell victim to these desires of power, dominance, and sensuality. Wise people turn away when they see how much suffering comes from chasing pleasures.

"The cravings don't end with getting what you want—the fire of desire simply moves on to newer cravings, leading to more problems. It's like being drunk on success. This leads people to do immoral things, which eventually causes their downfall. Why would anyone enjoy pleasures that require so much work to get and keep? They're temporary joys that end in disappointment.

"These pleasures are like holding a burning coal—the more you grasp them, the more they burn. Excessive indulgence in comfort and pleasures brings misery even to gods. People who get caught up in pleasures never find lasting peace—it's like being bitten by a poisonous snake, where the pain lasts far longer than the surface wound. People are never satisfied with pleasures—they're like hungry dogs chewing on dry bones, getting no real nourishment.

"Someone who becomes blinded by pleasure becomes a slave to wanting more and more. They might as well be dead while living. Just as deer are trapped by hunters' songs, insects die in flames, and fish are caught by bait—pleasures lead people to suffering.

"It's wrong to think that pleasures bring real happiness. Nice clothes and luxury items just help us avoid discomfort—they don't bring true joy. Think about it: we drink water because we're thirsty, eat because we're hungry, live in houses to stay safe from weather, and wear clothes to stay warm and decent. We sleep because we're tired, use vehicles because walking is hard, sit down to rest our legs, and bathe to stay clean and healthy. The things we own just help us avoid pain—they don't give us real happiness.

"Would you say taking medicine is enjoyment? Think about someone with a fever using a cold compress—they're not experiencing pleasure, they're just relieving pain. This same idea applies to all pleasures in life. Nothing that gives us pleasure lasts forever. In fact, the same things that make us feel good can also cause us pain. Warm clothes and scented wood feel nice in winter but become uncomfortable in summer. Moonlight and cooling sandal paste are pleasant in hot weather but unpleasant when it's cold.

"In life, good and bad experiences always come together—like two sides of a coin. That's why no one stays completely happy or completely sad forever. When you understand how pleasure and pain are connected, you realize there's not much difference between being a king or being a slave. Kings aren't always happy, and slaves aren't always suffering. Being a king actually brings more worries because of the huge responsibilities.

"Like a thin thread holding up a heavy knife over his head, a king carries the burden of caring for their whole kingdom. A king faces two problems: If they trust in their power too much, they'll suffer when their ministers and military generals revolt. But if they can't trust in their power, how can they ever exert influence? Even if a king rules the whole world, they can only live in one place and sleep in one bed. Isn't being a king just working hard for others' benefit?

"When you think about it, even a king only needs basic things—clothes, food, a bed, and a chair. Everything else is just for show. All these royal privileges aren't meant to make anyone happy; I can find happiness without them. Once you're truly content, do these extra things really matter? Someone who has found real happiness can't be fooled by temporary pleasures.

"As your friend, I ask you: are these pleasures really worth anything? I didn't leave my home because I was angry or defeated. I'm not refusing your offer because I'm looking for something better. Only a fool would grab a poisonous snake after letting it go, or pick up a burning torch after dropping it. That's what it would be like to chase after pleasures after giving them up.

"Only someone very confused would envy those who are worse off—like a person with eyesight envying the blind, or a free person envying a prisoner. That's how foolish it is to envy people who are caught up in worldly pleasures.

"My friend, someone who lives simply by accepting donations doesn't need your pity. They've found true happiness and peace, and won't face suffering in the future. Actually, we should feel sorry for the wealthy person who always wants more. They can't find peace in this life, and their endless wanting will lead to pain in the next life.

"Dear King Bimbisara, what you've offered out of your kindness matches who you are and how you live. And my choice matches who I am and how I want to live. I've seen how much struggle there is in the world, and now I just want peace. I wouldn't even accept a kingdom in heaven to escape life's problems—so why would I want an earthly kingdom?

"King, you talked about how everyone should pursue pleasure, wealth, and power, saying my path will bring suffering. But these things you value don't last and never truly satisfy. You suggested I wait until I'm old to be spiritual, saying young people always change their minds. But that doesn't make sense—old people can be uncertain while young people can be determined. Death can come at any time, at any age. So why should a wise person who wants peace wait until they're old? Death is like a hunter, using old age and sickness as weapons to strike down all living things. Knowing this, who would want to live longer just to chase worldly pleasures?

"The path of kindness and spirituality is right for everyone—young, old, or child. They should start as soon as they understand this truth.

"You talked about performing religious sacrifices, saying they suit my royal background and bring rewards. I respect these traditions, but I don't want rewards that come from causing others pain. It would be wrong for someone who cares about others to kill helpless creatures, even if it promised eternal rewards.

"True religion should be about self-control, good behavior, and freedom from harmful desires. It's wrong to follow rules that say we must kill to get the highest rewards. Wise and compassionate people hate the idea of gaining happiness by hurting others in this life—and it's even worse to do it for rewards in a future life.

"King, I can't be tempted by promises of future rewards. I'm not interested in being born again. These promises are as uncertain as plants being beaten down by heavy rain."

The king put his hands together respectfully and said, "Siddhartha, you are wise beyond your years. Feel free to follow your path. When you've achieved what you're seeking, please come back to visit me so that I can learn from you." After Gautama promised to visit again someday, the king and his officials went back to the palace.

Five ascetic spiritual seekers met Gautama in Rajagriha and asked him about his spiritual search. They brought good news from his homeland, Kapilavastu. After he left, the people had used peaceful protests to stop a war with the Koliyas. Now both sides were peacefully working out how to share their water. The seekers suggested Gautama should return home, since the war was now averted, but Siddhartha remained steadfast in his decision to be a monk, explaining he needed to continue his journey as he felt his calling was to end suffering. When they invited him to join their strict ascetic religious practices, he declined and spent time thinking alone.

He began to doubt himself: "Why did I leave my people in the first place? Since there's peace now, should I go back home?" But then he understood that his mission had become about something bigger. "There are conflicts everywhere—between communities, within families, and inside each person. These conflicts are what make people suffer. Even though the conflict at home was avoided, I still need to find an answer to why people fight within themselves and others and suffer." With this clear purpose in mind, he decided to continue searching for answers on his own.

He heard there was a great meditation master "Arada Kalam" who taught "Sankhya Philosophy" in the city of Vaishali & sought to visit him to seek answers to his questions.

Chapter 5

Study of various prevailing Philosophies

During his journey to Vaishali city, Gautama stopped at Brighu's hermitage. There, he encountered Brahmin priests practicing extreme fasting—some ate only wild plants, others consumed grass, and some attempted to survive on air alone. They believed these harsh ascetic practices would grant them entry to heaven and invited Siddhartha to join them. Gautama politely explained that his interest lay in finding a way to end suffering on earth, rather than earning heavenly rewards. He then proceeded to Vindhyakoshtha to study Sankhya Philosophy. Upon reaching Kalam's teaching center in Vaishali, Gautama received a warm welcome. Kalam, impressed by Gautama's good character, taught him the Sankhya teachings, which Gautama quickly grasped and found beneficial.

Learning Sankhya Philosophy

Kapila was one of the most important thinkers in ancient India. He created a way of thinking called Sankhya Philosophy that differed from other philosophers of his time. His ideas were based on simple yet important principles. The most fundamental was that *every claim needs proof—you can't just believe something* without evidence.

He proposed only two ways to prove things: **Direct observation or Stepwise logical reasoning**. He explained these concepts using everyday examples.

Direct observation means reaching conclusions using your senses of sight, hearing, smell, taste, and touch.

Logical reasoning works in three ways:

1. Stepwise anticipation of future events based on past experiences (like predicting rain when seeing dark clouds)

2. Determining present causes by tracing past events (like deducing it rained in the mountains when rivers rise today)

3. Understanding phenomena by comparing observations across space and time (like realizing stars move because their positions change, similar to how people move)

Kapila's view of universe creation differed from his contemporaries. Rather than believing in a divine creator, he argued that *everything must come from something that already existed*—just as a clay pot comes from clay, or cloth from thread. His logic was straightforward: something that doesn't exist cannot suddenly begin acting. Everything we see is merely existing materials arranged in new ways. He emphasized that specific materials can only create specific things—you cannot make something from just any material.

Kapila explained the universe's workings through a dual classification: things that have already developed (like plants, animals, and visible objects), and things yet to develop into their final form. He reasoned that individual visible objects couldn't be the original source of everything, as they're too limited—like how a single tree couldn't be the source of all trees. There must be something more fundamental.

While everything comes from something else, Kapila proposed an *ultimate source that exists independently*. When questioned about why this source couldn't be detected, he offered practical explanations: it might be too small, too distant, hidden, or mixed with other things. He drew parallels to how we know certain things exist despite being unable to see them. This ultimate source, he explained, differs from everything else—it is infinite and omnipresent, unlike limited physical objects. While physical objects have parts and functions, this source simply exists without action. Kapila described three basic forces for this source.

1. Sattva—brings light and happiness

2. Rajas—creates movement and action

3. Tamas—produces slowness and stillness

These forces work in harmony, like a lamp's flame, oil, and wick. When perfectly balanced, the universe remains calm and unchanging. Imbalance in these forces, which Kapila attributed to worldly suffering, triggers change and evolution. These ideas formed the core tenets of Kapila's philosophy. The Buddha particularly admired Kapila's teachings, considering him the only philosopher whose doctrines were firmly grounded in the logic and facts of their time.

However, the Buddha did not accept all of Kapila's teachings. He embraced just three key principles:

First, that reality must rest on proof and thinking must be based on rationalism.

Second, that there was no logical or factual basis for believing in God's existence or role as creator of the universe.

Third, that Dukha (suffering) exists in the world.

Learning Dhyana marga (Path of Meditation)

During his search for truth, Gautama studied different ways to train his mind through meditation (Dhyana). He learned three main types of breathing exercises:

1. Mindful breathing (Anapanasati) — paying careful attention to your breath during everyday activities

2. Controlled breathing (Pranayama) — a three-part process of breathing in, holding the breath, and breathing out

3. Deep meditation (Samadhi) — reaching a state of complete concentration on a single object

Gautama first studied meditation and Sankhya philosophy under Arada Kalam, who taught him a seven-step meditation method. Though Gautama quickly mastered all steps, he felt there was more to learn and moved on. His next teacher, Uddaka Ramaputta, offered an advanced eight-step meditation technique. Again, Gautama swiftly mastered the practice but remained unfulfilled in his search.

After mastering these high-level meditation practices and finding himself no closer to solving the problem of suffering, Gautama traveled to the city of Magadha. There, he learned their unique meditation practice focusing on prolonged breath retention. Despite experiencing physical pain, severe headaches, and loud ringing in his ears, Gautama mastered this technique as well. Yet even after conquering all these methods, Gautama remained unsatisfied—they neither revealed truth nor helped reduce human suffering. He continued his search.

Practise of extreme Asceticism

After studying Sankhya and Samadhi Marga, Gautama decided to explore Asceticism to understand it firsthand. He settled in Uruvela, a secluded spot by the Nairanjana river near Gaya, at Negari's hermitage. There he reunited with the five Parivrajakas from Rajagraha, who became his devoted pupils.

Gautama practiced extreme austerities, limiting himself to visiting between two and seven houses daily, accepting only two to seven morsels of food at each. He restricted himself to one small bowl of food per day, never exceeding seven bowls per week. As he progressed in his austere practices, he would eat only once daily, then once every two days, extending this pattern until he ate just once every fortnight. His diet became increasingly sparse—consisting only of wild herbs, millet grains, water plants, rice husks, discarded rice scum, or oilseed flour. He sustained himself on nothing but wild roots, fruits, and fallen food. His clothing was equally austere: hemp cloth, discarded rags, tree bark, antelope hide, grass, wooden strips, or blankets woven from human or animal hair and owl feathers. In his dedication to asceticism, he would pluck out his head and facial hair. He refused to lie down, remaining only in squatting or standing positions.

He tortured his body through various harsh practices, allowing dirt and filth to accumulate on his skin until it fell away naturally. He made his home in the most fearsome parts of the forest—places so terrifying that it was said only the foolhardy would enter without trembling. During the cold season, he spent his nights in the open air and his days in dense thickets. In the scorching summer months before the monsoon, he reversed this pattern—exposing himself to the burning sun by day and retreating to stifling thickets at night. He chose to sleep in cremation grounds, using charred bones as his pillow.

His fasting became even more extreme—surviving on just a single bean, sesame seed, or grain of rice each day. Living on a single piece of fruit daily, his body became severely emaciated. When he touched his stomach, he could feel his backbone, and when reaching for his spine, he found his belly—so completely had his body wasted away from lack of nourishment. For six long years, Gautama practiced the most extreme forms of self-denial and physical hardship. By the end of this time, his body had become so weak he could barely move. Despite all this suffering, he hadn't found any answers to his central question: how to end the suffering that exists within us & in the world.

After deep reflection, he came to several important realizations: "This path of extreme physical hardship isn't working," he thought. "It's not leading to inner peace, wisdom, or freedom."

"People everywhere put themselves through different kinds of suffering - some for worldly gains, others hoping for rewards in heaven. But in their desperate search for happiness, they only find more pain. Haven't I done the same thing?" "It's not that trying hard is wrong - there's nothing wrong with pursuing a higher purpose. But I have to ask myself: Is hurting my body really the path to spiritual truth?" "The body only does what the mind tells it to do. *So isn't it more important to control our thoughts? Without the mind's guidance, the body is useless -* like a dog without its master."

"Eating pure food might bring some benefit the body, and for the mind to function optimally, we need to take care of the body. What's the point if the person is too weak to think clearly? How can someone find new wisdom when they're exhausted from hunger, thirst, and physical strain? When the mind is tired, it can't think properly. And how can anyone reach spiritual peace when their mind isn't calm? To truly calm and control the mind, we need to take care of our body's basic needs."

In the village of Uruvela, there lived a man named Senani and his daughter Sujata. She had once prayed to a Banyan Tree, promising to make food offerings if she had a son. When her wish came true, she kept her promise. One day, Sujata sent her servant Punna to prepare for the offering. When Punna found Gautama sitting under the Banyan Tree, He reported that a divine being is sitting under the tree. Sujatha revered him as the tree's divine spirit who had come down to earth. Sujata brought food in a golden bowl and offered it to Gautama. He went to the riverbank, bathed at a place called Suppatitthita, and ate the food. This marked the end of his time practicing extreme ascetic self-denial.

The five ascetics who had been following Gautama were unhappy with his decision to stop his harsh self denying lifestyle by eating a single bowl of food. They felt disappointed and left him.

Chapter 6

Mara's Defeat & Enlightenment

After finishing his meal, Gautama reflected on his previous attempts at finding spiritual truth. Although disappointed by these failed attempts, he remained hopeful of finding the path out of suffering. That night, he had five dreams that he interpreted as auspicious signs about his path to enlightenment. To test whether he was on the right path, he took the bowl Sujata had given him and cast it into the Nairanja river, declaring that if he was truly meant to reach enlightenment, the bowl would float upstream. The bowl did float against the current briefly before sinking. Encouraged by this sign, he journeyed to Gaya, where he found a Banyan Tree. Following the tradition of great spiritual teachers before him, he sat facing east and began to meditate beneath it.

Seated cross-legged and upright under the Banyan Tree, Gautama made a powerful declaration: "Let my skin, sinews, and bones dry up; let my flesh and blood waste away—but I will not leave this seat until I have attained complete enlightenment." As he meditated, he wrestled with self-doubts about his worthiness to discover universal truths that had eluded so many great men before him. Later stories dramatized these doubts as a battle with a demon called Mara, a figure similar to Satan in Christian tradition. Mara represented all that prevents inner peace—attachment to worldly desires and pursuit of fleeting pleasures.

During Buddha's meditation, Mara tested him with desires, anger, hunger, fatigue, and self-doubt, attempting to break his concentration. Though other celestial beings witnessed this momentous event, they fled at Mara's appearance, leaving Buddha to face these challenges alone. Yet Gautama confronted these negative thoughts induced by Mara, declaring: "I have faith, courage, and wisdom. How can you defeat me? Even if the wind could dry up rivers, you cannot break my determination. I would rather die fighting than live in defeat."

In another version of the story, Mara attempted to break Buddha's focus by sending his beautiful daughters to tempt him, but Buddha remained unmoved. When this failed, Mara questioned Buddha's right to sit immovably under the sacred tree. Buddha calmly explained that he had earned his place through good actions, kindness to others, and dedication to spiritual growth. When Mara boasted that his vast army could prove his own deeds and challenged Buddha to find a witness to his good works, Buddha responded with a simple yet powerful gesture—he reached down and touched the ground, asking the Earth itself to be his witness. This ***"earth-touching gesture" (bhumi-sparsa-mudra)*** became significant in Buddhist tradition and is frequently depicted in Buddha statues today. The story tells that upon Buddha's earth-touch,

Mara's power dissolved—he fell from his elephant as his armies scattered.

Having gathered provisions for forty days of meditation, Gautama first overcame Mara before taking nourishment to restore his strength. Thus fortified, he began his meditation toward enlightenment.

Through four weeks of deep practice, he progressed through distinct stages: first cultivating reason and investigation in seclusion, then developing concentration, followed by attaining equanimity and mindfulness. In the final stage, he refined these qualities—deepening his mindfulness and achieving pure equanimity. His mind became concentrated, pure, and unblemished—free from impurity, flexible, steady, firm, and detached. With this clarity, Gautama focused intently on his fundamental question: "How could suffering be eliminated?"

After 49 days of meditation, darkness yielded to light, and ignorance gave way to wisdom. He had discovered a new path. He approached this systematically, first examining the causes of suffering and unhappiness, then contemplating their removal. Through his meditation, he found answers to both questions—achieving what became known as ***"Samma Bodhi" (Right Enlightenment)***. This profound realization led to his meditation site becoming known as the Bodhi Tree. After reaching enlightenment, Buddha faced a big decision: should he teach others what he had learned?

What he found with his enlightenment was contrarian to so many prevailing ideas of his time. The people might have a very difficult time Changing what they believed about God, giving up their old religious habits, understanding karma in a new way, accepting that there isn't an eternal soul, and learning to think of others instead of just themselves. At first, Buddha thought it might be easier to just live alone as a holy man and focus on his own spiritual journey.

Then a divine being named Brahma Sahampati noticed Buddha's doubts. He came to Buddha and said: "The world needs your wisdom. *You're not just Siddharth Gautama anymore—you're the Buddha, the Enlightened One*. How can you not help humanity? People are suffering because they haven't heard what you've learned. Look at all the suffering people below. Stand up, great hero, and show them the way. Please teach both humans and gods."

Buddha answered: "I wasn't sure about teaching because I thought it would be too hard for people to understand." But then Buddha realized something important: there was too much unhappiness in the world for him to just sit back and do nothing. He understood that trying to escape from the world's problems through isolation wasn't the answer. Instead of staying away from the world, he needed to return and help make it better. He remembered why he had left his royal life in the first place—because he saw so much suffering and didn't know how to fix it. Now that he had found a way to reduce suffering through his teachings, he knew it was his duty to share this knowledge with others rather than remain silent.

In the end, Buddha accepted Brahma's request and decided to teach his ideas to the world. Pleased with convincing Buddha to teach, Brahma Sahampati bowed, circled him, and departed. As he left, he proclaimed: "Rejoice! The Buddha has found the source of suffering and knows the path to end it. He will bring comfort to the weary, peace to those in conflict, and hope to the oppressed. His teachings offer love to the unloved, dignity to the degraded, and equality to the downtrodden. His doctrine is one of truth, reason, and righteousness. Blessed is the Buddha who teaches the middle way, peace of Nibbana, and the path of love and kindness to help all beings find salvation."

After Buddha decided to teach others, he first wanted to find his five old friends who had practiced asceticism with him near the Niranjana river. "These friends helped me a lot in the past," he thought. When he learned they were staying at a deer park called Isipatana in Sarnath, he went to see them. At first, his five friends were upset with Buddha because he had stopped following their strict ascetic way of life. They agreed among themselves not to give him a warm welcome.

But when Buddha arrived, something amazing happened—his presence was so powerful and radiant that they forgot their anger. Instead, they welcomed him warmly, helped him with his things, and even brought water to wash his feet. What started as an unfriendly welcome turned into deep respect.

Chapter 7

Majjhima Patipada- The Middle Path

After exchanging greetings, the five Parivrajakas asked Buddha if he still believed in asceticism. Buddha replied that he did not. He explained that life presents two extremes: complete indulgence in pleasure and severe self-denial. One extreme says, "Let us eat and drink, for tomorrow we die," while the other demands severe self-denial of all bodily needs and elimination of all desires (vasanas), claiming these cause rebirth. Buddha rejected both paths as unworthy of human nature. Instead, he taught the ***Madhyama Marga (Majjhima Patipada)—the middle path that avoids both extreme worldly indulgence and extreme self-mortification.***

Buddha asked the Parivrajakas, "If worldly or heavenly pleasures still mentally tempt you, isn't physical self-denial completely futile? How can harsh self-denial free you from desires if it doesn't address the root of your wants?"

He continued, "True freedom comes only when you've overcome selfish desires. Then you can meet your basic needs without being controlled by them. You should nourish your body with what it needs to stay healthy. Chasing pleasures weakens you. Someone who lives only for pleasure becomes a slave to their desires. But I'm telling you that taking care of your basic needs isn't wrong - in fact, keeping your body healthy is important. Without a healthy body, you can't keep your mind clear and strong for wisdom."

"Listen carefully: there are two extremes people shouldn't follow. The first is constantly giving in to desires and pleasures - this is an unworthy path that brings no real benefit. The second is harsh self-denial and punishment of the body - this is also harmful and pointless. Instead, there is a middle path between these extremes. This is the path I teach." The five Parivrajakas listened carefully to Buddha's words.

They weren't sure how to respond to this idea of a middle path, so they asked what he had done after leaving them. Buddha explained how he went to Gaya and meditated under the Banyan Tree for four weeks. During this time, he reached enlightenment and discovered a new way of living. Hearing this, the Parivrajakas were eager to learn more and asked Buddha to explain this path to them. Buddha's teachings, called ***Dhamma***, were unique. Rather than focusing on theological concepts, he emphasized practical wisdom.

He focused on human relationships and daily life interactions. Most importantly, he addressed suffering. Seeing widespread hardship and sadness, *Buddha believed spiritual teachings should have one purpose:* ***ending suffering.*** *Without this goal, he considered teachings meaningless.*

The Parivrajakas (his followers) then asked him an important question: "If your teaching is about ending suffering, how exactly does it do that?"

Buddha answered that suffering could end if everyone followed three simple paths:

1. The Path of Purity

2. The Eightfold Path of Righteousness (Ashtanga Marga)

3. The Path of Virtue

He told them that he had found these paths himself and knew they worked.

Chapter 8
The Path of Purity

The Parivrajakas asked Buddha to explain his Dhamma further, and he gladly agreed. He began by discussing the Path of Purity.

"The Path of Purity teaches that a person who wishes to be good must recognize certain foundational standards for living.

These standards are: do not injure or kill, do not steal or take what belongs to others, do not speak lies, do not indulge in lust, and do not partake of intoxicating drinks.

These principles are essential for everyone, as they provide a standard by which to judge one's actions. People everywhere may stray from the path, but there are two kinds: *those who have moral standards and those who have none*.

Those without standards cannot recognize their fallen state and thus remain there. Those with standards, however, strive to rise again because they recognize when they have strayed. This distinction between having standards and having none is crucial. What matters most is not that someone has fallen, but whether they have principles to guide them back.

"You may ask why these principles deserve recognition as life standards. Consider two questions: Do these principles benefit the individual? Do they promote the good of society?

If both answers are yes, then the Path of Purity stands as a true standard for life."

The parivrajakas unanimously agreed.

Chapter 9

Eightfold Path of Righteousness (Ashtanga Marga)

The Buddha continued, "Once our lives are set on the path of purity through foundational standards by which we live, we must develop righteousness to uphold those standards. For this, we follow the eightfold path of righteousness."

Samma Ditthi (Right Understanding)

He began his discourse with the exposition of Samma Ditti, the first and foremost element in the Ashtangmarga. "Think of it this way: Most people are living in a dark room. They can't see clearly and don't even realize they're stuck in darkness, like fish swimming in a river unaware of the water. They've been in the dark so long that they might not even believe light exists. Our mind is like a window that lets in light, but most people's minds only let in a tiny bit—just enough to show them they're in darkness. However, there's hope. Everyone has willpower inside them. When we find the right path, we can use this willpower to improve our understanding of life and the world around us, making changes to avoid suffering from thoughts generated by the untrained mind.

As we let more light of understanding into our minds, we can start moving toward freedom. We can begin this journey right now, as I am showing you the path. Our mind is like a muscle —we can train it to work differently. While our mind might trap us in certain habitual ways of thinking, it can also free us when we learn to use it properly.

The main goal of Samma Ditti is the destruction of Avijja (ignorance). Ignorance here means not understanding basic truths about why we suffer and how we can stop suffering. To develop Samma Ditti, we need to let go of superstitions and supernatural beliefs, stop accepting ideas that aren't based on facts or real experience, and keep our minds open and think freely.

Samma Sankappa (Right Thought)

Everyone has aims, aspirations, and ambitions. Samma Sankappo teaches that these goals should be noble and praiseworthy, directed toward the highest good for the longest timeframe possible, rather than selfish, narrow, ignoble, and unworthy. The Buddha's main teaching focused on compassion and training the mind.

Everything starts with the mind. If you train the mind to have only good thoughts, happiness follows like a cart follows a horse. If you do not train the mind properly and it harbors unhappy, unproductive, craving thoughts, unhappiness follows like a cart after the horse.

Samma Sankappa states : "Train your mind to have only pure thoughts working toward selfless, lofty goals. Everything begins there."

Samma Vacca (Right speech)

Samma vacca (Right Speech) means: Always tell the truth and be honest in all communication. Avoid gossip and speaking ill of others. Speak with kindness and compassion, using gentle, measured words instead of harsh or angry ones. Speak mindfully—ensure your words are meaningful and beneficial. Right Speech should come from genuine integrity, not from fear of consequences or desire for reward.

Your truthful and kind speech should not depend on who is listening or what you might gain.

Practice Right Speech simply because it is the correct path.

Samma Kamanto (Right behaviour / Right actions)

Samma Kamanto teaches that all our actions and behavior should be based on respect for others' welfare and rights. Our conduct should align with the fundamental laws that govern all beings' natural existence, guided by a deep appreciation of our present life. When our actions harmonize with these laws of existence and we take energetic action to alleviate suffering, we affirm all earthly life and follow Samma Kamanto.

Samma Ajiva (Right livelihood)

Everyone must earn a living, but not all ways of earning are equal. Poverty is one of the greatest sources of suffering, and earning a livelihood to support ourselves and our families is essential to escape it. Living in poverty while pursuing spiritual growth serves no virtuous purpose and benefits no one. We must first meet our basic bodily needs before we can focus on training the mind. In pursuing our livelihood, we must choose ethical paths that avoid causing harm or injustice to others. We should seek ways to support ourselves and our families while respecting all living beings. This is Samma Ajivo (Right Livelihood).

Samma Vyayamo (Right Endeavour / Effort)

Samma Vyayamo (Right Endeavour) is the primary effort to train the mind to remove Avijja (ignorance)—the key to escaping this cycle of suffering. It focuses on four purposes: (1) To prevent harmful states of mind from arising that conflict with the Ashtangamarga; (2) To swiftly overcome harmful states that have already arisen; (3) To develop positive states of mind that support following the Ashtangamarga; and (4) To maintain and strengthen these positive states to remain in Samma Ditti & Samma Sankapa once developed. Samma Vyayamo serves as the shield that prevents the mind from moving into Avijja.

Samma Sati (Right mindfulness / Awareness)

Samma Sati means being mindful and aware of where our attention flows. The mind is like a ploughed field, and attention is like a moving river. The mind remains immobile—only our awareness moves through it. We can direct our moment-to-moment awareness toward either good or bad. While remodeling the mind through the Dhamma is a long-term process, directing our attention is a moment-to-moment task.

We must maintain a strong grip on our awareness in every moment we are alive, directing it solely toward the ashtanga marga. Samma Sati teaches us to gently and lovingly bring our awareness back to the path of purity when we notice it flowing into greed, hatred, or ignorance.

As our awareness moves through the mind, thoughts and impulses occupy our consciousness and lead to speech or actions. We should steward our awareness so that everything is directed toward the highest good possible. This requires maintaining constant mental alertness—watching over the mind, guarding against negative impulses while directing our attention toward the highest good of compassion and love.

Samma Samadhi (Right Concentration / Focus)

There are five fetters or hindrances that block a person from achieving the ashtangamargha. These five hindrances are covetousness, ill-will, sloth and torpor, doubt, and indecision. To overcome these fetters, one must practice Samma Samadhi. Samadhi refers to concentration. Intense concentration while doing a single task can lead to self-induced meditative states *(Dhyanic states / Flow states)* that temporarily suspend the five hindrances, these states don't last. What we truly need is a permanent transformation of the mind, which only Samma Samadhi can provide.

Regular Samadhi has limitations—it merely suspends hindrances temporarily without training the mind. Samma Samadhi, however, takes a positive approach. It trains the mind to focus on Kusala Kamma (Good Deeds and Thoughts) during concentration, eliminating its tendency to drift toward Akusala Kamma (Bad Deeds and Bad Thoughts) that arise from these hindrances. *Samma Samadhi states our need to develop intense Laser like focus to doing only Kusala Kamma.*

Chapter 10

The Path of Virtue (Paramithas)

The Buddha then explained to the Parivrajakas the Tenfold Path of Virtue. He taught that the path of virtue requires observing ten essential virtues. When the Parivrajakas asked him to explain these virtues, Buddha described them:

1. ***Sila*** is moral character—the disposition to do good and avoid evil, coupled with a sense of shame at wrongdoing. It represents an inner moral compass that guides one away from harmful actions.

2. ***Nekkhama*** is the renunciation of worldly pleasures.

3. ***Dana*** is selfless giving—offering one's possessions, effort, and even life to benefit others without expecting anything in return.

4. ***Virya*** is energetic action —pursuing your chosen path with complete commitment, never retreating. 5. "Khanti is forbearance. Its essence lies in refusing to meet hatred with hatred, recognizing that hatred can only be calmed through patience and understanding.

6. ***Succa*** is truthfulness. One must speak only what is true, making truth the foundation of all speech.

7. ***Adhithana*** is resolute determination to reach the goal.

8. ***Karuna*** is loving-kindness toward all human beings.

9. ***Maitri*** is extending fellowship to all beings—not merely to friends but also to foes, not just to humans but to all living creatures.

10. ***Uppekha*** is true detachment, distinct from mere indifference. It is a balanced state of mind free from both attraction and aversion, remaining engaged while unattached to outcomes. "These virtues must be practiced to their fullest extent. This is why they are called Paramitas—States of Perfection."

Importance of Prajna Paramitha

After explaining his teachings, Buddha asked his followers: "Isn't being a good person—having purity of character—the foundation of all good things in the world? Don't negative traits like greed, excessive desires, ignorance, and harmful actions make it harder to be good? Don't we need to build strong character to overcome these behaviors? How can anyone help others without first developing goodness within themselves?

"Why do some people accept the domination and suffering of others? Isn't it because they've abandoned the principle of treating others fairly?

"If everyone followed the Ashtanga marga—practicing right views, truthful speech, honest work, and mindfulness—wouldn't that eliminate the unfairness and cruelty people show to each other? Don't we need generosity to help those who suffer? Don't we need compassion to inspire our service to others? Don't we need selflessness to do good work? Don't we need perseverance even when there's no personal gain?

"Isn't love and compassion for others essential?" His followers agreed. "But love alone isn't enough. We need friendship and kindness toward all living beings, not just humans. Don't we need this universal love? What else can help us treat all beings with the same care we desire for ourselves, maintaining equanimity and goodwill toward everyone?

"However, when we practice these virtues, we must also apply wisdom. Universal Compassion (Paramitha) should always be accompanied by Wisdom (Prajna)." When Buddha asked why wisdom was necessary, his followers were quiet.

To help them understand, he explained: "A good person avoids harmful actions in deed, thought, speech, and livelihood. But should we practice goodness without understanding? No. If that were enough, we could say a baby is perfectly good. A baby only knows how to move its body, not its purpose. It can only cry, not speak. It can only feel, not think. It can only feed from its mother, not sustain itself. This is why we must apply wisdom and understanding in our pursuit of goodness.

"There's another reason wisdom is essential. Without wisdom, even generosity can cause harm. Without wisdom, compassion might enable wrongdoing. Every virtuous action must be guided by wisdom. We must understand what makes actions right or wrong, and how harmful actions arise. We must also understand what truly constitutes good. Without this understanding, something might appear good but not be genuinely beneficial. That's why wisdom is indispensable while being compassionate."

Finally, Buddha concluded: "You might think my teachings are negative because they address suffering. But this isn't true. While I discuss suffering, I also reveal the path to freedom. My teachings offer both hope and purpose—they help people understand suffering and show the way to end it."

The five Parivrajakas immediately recognized this as a truly new Dhamma. Deeply moved by this novel approach to life's challenges, they declared unanimously: "Never in history has anyone taught that understanding human suffering is the true foundation of existence and that removing this misery is its ultimate purpose! Never before has a path to salvation been presented that is so straightforward, so free from supernatural elements, so independent of—even opposed to—beliefs in soul, God, and afterlife! Never before has a framework emerged from examining present human social needs rather than divine revelation, with principles founded on reason rather than divine commands!

"Never before has salvation been conceived as happiness attainable by humans in this life, on this earth, through righteousness born of their own efforts!"

They recognized in him a reformer of profound moral purpose, well-versed in the intellectual culture of his time, who had the originality and courage to present—while fully aware of opposing viewpoints—a doctrine of salvation achievable in this life through inner transformation, brought about by training the mind, right speech, right actions and self-control.

Deeply moved, they asked to become his disciples, and Buddha welcomed them with "Ehi Bhikkave" (come in Bhikkus). These became the ***Panchavargiya Bhikkus. (The first disciples of Buddha)***

Chapter 11

Spreading of the Dhamma doctrine

After explaining the Dhamma doctrine as the cure for human suffering, the Buddha welcomed distinguished men into his order of Sangha, including the Yashas, King Bimbisara, King Pasenjit, and many others.

When teaching the Kashyapas, who were fire-worshipping Rishis, the Buddha explained: "The dark smoke of ignorance rises, and confused thoughts—like wood drilled into wood—create the fire. Lust, anger, and delusion are flames that burn all things, bringing grief and sorrow to the world. When one finds this path and extinguishes lust, anger, and delusion, then sight, knowledge, and pure conduct emerge. As the heart develops distaste for sin, this aversion removes covetous desire. When covetous desire is extinguished, peace follows." Upon hearing this teaching, the great Rishis abandoned their fire worship and became the Buddha's disciples.

Should we really become a homeless monk to follow the path of Buddha?

The treasurer to King Pasenjit of Kosala, Anathapindika came to meet Buddha. Seeing his pure heart, Buddha warmly welcomed him and agreed to share his teachings.

Buddha began by asking an important question: "Who controls our lives? Some say it's God. But consider this—if God made everything, wouldn't we all be like clay pots with no choice of our own? And if God created the world, why is there suffering and evil? Since both good and bad things would have to come from God, this creates a contradiction. Moreover, if other causes exist besides God, then God cannot be all-powerful. This reasoning shows why this idea is flawed."

Buddha continued, "Everything we see comes from a specific cause—like how a plant grows from a seed. If God is present in everything, how can God be the creator of everything? This, too, is contradictory."

"Some say that our 'self' and 'free will' creates everything in our lives. But this fails to explain reality—if we created everything and guided our lives entirely through free will, wouldn't we choose only pleasant experiences? Yet we experience both happiness and sadness, and these feelings are genuine. How could we have created them ourselves? And if we say there's no creator and things happen randomly, why would our choices matter?"

So here's what we believe: everything that happens has a cause. But the cause isn't God, a universal force, our individual self, or mere chance. Instead, our actions create good or bad results. ***Everything in the world follows this***

simple rule of cause and effect. Just as a gold cup is made entirely of gold, our actions shape everything that happens. Our actions shape even how we feel. So instead of wasting time pondering gods or getting lost in complex theories, let's focus on letting go of selfishness. Since everything happens for a reason, we should do good things so that good results will follow.

After hearing this, Anathapindika said, "I understand and want to learn more. What should I do? As a busy and wealthy businessman, I have many responsibilities and employees depending on me. Must I give up my wealth, home, and business to find spiritual happiness like you have?"

The Buddha answered: "Anyone can find spiritual happiness by following the eightfold path. If you're too cravingly attached to your wealth, it's better to give it up before it poisons your mind. But if you're not attached to it and use your wealth to help others, you can be a blessing to people."

"My advice is this: keep your current life and work hard at what you do. Remember—it's not having wealth and power that traps people, it's being too attached to them."

"A Bhikku who retires from the world only to lead an idle slothful life, being of no use to others, will gain nothing. Such indolence is an abomination, and lack of energy deserves contempt."

"My teachings don't require you to become homeless or leave regular life behind—you only need to do that if you truly feel it's your calling. What matters most is freeing yourself from selfish thinking, developing a pure heart, stopping the endless chase for pleasures, and living a good, moral life."

Whether you work as a craftsperson, business owner, government official, or choose to become a religious meditation teacher—what matters most is giving it your all. Work hard and stay determined. Be like a lotus flower—though it grows in muddy water, it remains clean and beautiful. Face life's challenges without succumbing to jealousy or anger. If you live focusing on truth rather than just yourself, you'll find real happiness, peace, and contentment in your life." Moved by Buddha's simple yet profound teachings, Anathapindika bowed and became his lay follower. Discourse with King Pasenjit

After Anathapindika was enraptured by the Buddha's Dhamma, King Pasenjit also wished to hear it. He visited the Buddha and requested counsel. The Buddha said, "Worldly profit is fleeting and perishable, but spiritual profit is eternal and inexhaustible. A worldly man, even a king, is full of trouble, while a holy common man has peace of mind."

Knowing the king's heart was weighed down by avarice and love of pleasure, the Buddha said: "Even those of humble birth feel reverence when they see a virtuous person—how much more should an independent king who has earned merit through previous lives?

"As I share these teachings, let the Maharaja listen carefully and hold fast to my words. Our good and evil deeds follow us as faithfully as shadows. Above all else, cultivate a loving heart! Care for your people as you would an only child. Never oppress or harm them. Keep your body and mind in check, abandon false doctrines, and follow the righteous path. Never elevate yourself by diminishing others. Bring comfort to those who suffer. Avoid dwelling on royal privileges or heeding flatterers' honeyed words.

"Self-torment through austerities brings no benefit—instead, meditate on Dhamma and contemplate the righteous law. The rocks of sorrow and suffering surround us, and only by following the true law can we escape this mountain of misery.

"What good can come from practicing injustice? The wise turn away from bodily pleasures, rejecting lust to seek spiritual growth.

"When flames consume a tree, how can birds find shelter there? Likewise, truth cannot exist where passion rules. Without understanding this, even the most learned person remains ignorant despite being praised as wise.

"True wisdom awakens in those who understand these teachings. Acquiring this wisdom is life's essential purpose—neglecting it renders life meaningless. All teachings must center on this truth, for without it, nothing has purpose. This wisdom belongs not only to hermits but to everyone—priests and laypeople alike. The distinction between monks and householders matters little. Some hermits may lose their way in darkness, while humble householders can rise to become sages.

"The flood of desire threatens all, sweeping away the world. Those caught in its current find no escape. Yet wisdom serves as our boat, and reflection our rudder. Religion calls us to overcome Mara, the enemy.

"Since we cannot escape our actions' consequences, let us perform good deeds.

"Let us examine our thoughts to avoid evil, knowing we reap what we sow.

"Some paths lead from light to darkness, others from darkness to light. While some paths descend deeper into gloom, others rise toward greater illumination. The wise use whatever light they possess to gain more light, steadily advancing toward truth.

"Demonstrate true excellence through virtuous conduct and reason; contemplate life's impermanence and understand its transient nature.

"Elevate your mind and pursue authentic faith with determination. Honor the principles of righteous leadership, and let your happiness spring from your mind rather than external things. This path will build your lasting legacy."

The king listened reverently, took the Blessed One's words to heart, and became his lay disciple.

Can Young & Wealthy too become Bhikkus? - Discourse of Bhikku Ratthapala with the Kuru King.

During a visit to the Kuru region, Buddha was staying in a town called Thullakotthita. After hearing him teach, a wealthy young man named Ratthapala wished to become a monk. Buddha told him he needed his parents' permission first. Though his parents initially refused, Ratthapala lay on the floor and refused food in protest until they agreed—on the condition that he would visit them later.

After becoming a monk and growing spiritually, Ratthapala returned to see his parents. At his father's house, they didn't recognize their son and were rude toward him. A servant girl recognized him and offered him rice. His father, upon realizing his mistake, went in search of his son. Finding him eating beneath a tree, the father invited him home and attempted to lure him back to secular life by offering wealth and showing him his former wives. Yet Ratthapala remained steadfast, explaining that wealth brings only suffering. After sharing one meal at his father's request, he returned to meditate in the deer park.

While preparing the park for the king's visit, a hunter discovered Ratthapala meditating under a tree. Upon hearing this, the king altered his plans to visit Ratthapala instead of touring the park. The king sat down and asked, "Ratthapala, people usually become monks for one of four reasons—they're either old, sick, poor, or have lost their family. But you're young, healthy, wealthy, and have a large family. So why did you choose to become a monk?"

"I became a monk," Ratthapala replied, "because I learned four important truths from the Buddha: (i) Everything in the world is impermanent. (ii) Our actions alone can protect or save us. (iii) We truly own nothing—we must leave everything behind in the end. (iv) People are never satisfied, as they are always craving more."

"It is wonderful, it is marvelous," exclaimed the king, "how right in this the Lord was!"

Chapter 12

Buddha's Father Sends Another Appeal

Suddhodhana sent a message through a courtier's son named Kaludayin. He asked Buddha to visit him before he died, saying that while many others had learned from Buddha's teachings, his own family had not. The messenger made a heartfelt plea, comparing Buddha's father to a flower waiting for the sun to rise. Buddha accepted the invitation and traveled home with his followers.

Word spread quickly through the Sakya region that Prince Siddharth was returning. His father Suddhodana and stepmother Mahaprajapati came out with their followers to greet him. When they finally saw Buddha, they were speechless. Though he looked like their son, he had transformed completely—he was now Buddha, a great teacher. His father dismounted his horse and bowed to him, noting tearfully that they hadn't seen each other for seven years. As they sat together, his father yearned to call him "Siddharth" as before but found he couldn't. In his heart, he wished for his son to return to his old life, but seeing Buddha's determination, he kept these thoughts to himself. He felt both proud and deeply saddened that his son would never rule the kingdom.

"I would give you my kingdom," Suddhodana said simply, "but I know you wouldn't want it."

The Buddha replied, "I know you love me deeply as your son and feel great sadness. But instead of directing all your love just toward me, share it with all living beings. In return, you'll gain something better than your son Siddharth—you'll find a teacher of truth who brings peace and enlightenment to your heart."

Suddhodana was moved by his son's wise words. With tears in his eyes and joined hands, he said, "What a wonderful change! My sadness is gone now. At first I felt heavy-hearted, but now I understand why you left. You made the right choice in giving up being a king to follow your spiritual journey. Now that you have found wisdom, you can help others find peace too."

The next morning, Buddha walked through the streets of Kapilavatsu seeking alms. People were astonished to see their former prince carrying a simple bowl, walking the same streets where he once rode in royal carriages. When Suddhodana learned of this, he rushed to Buddha, exclaiming, "Why are you doing this? I can provide you and your followers with all the food you need forever!"

"This is how we live," Buddha simply replied.

"But you never needed to ask for food before!"

"Father, you come from a line of kings, but I follow the way of all Buddhas before me—we live only on what people kindly give us."

The Blessed One continued, "It is customary, when one finds a hidden treasure, to offer the most precious jewel to one's father. Let me therefore offer you my greatest treasure—the Dhamma. If you free yourself from illusions, open your mind to truth, act with diligence, and practice righteousness, you will find eternal bliss."

Suddhodana heard these words in silence and replied, "My son, I will strive to fulfill what you say. But please come to your home and bless Yashodhara and your son Rahula."

Inside the palace, everyone welcomed Buddha respectfully, but his wife Yashodhara remained in her room, overcome with both joy and sadness. When Buddha entered, Yashodhara was so emotional that she fell at his feet crying. Upon noticing Buddha's father, she composed herself and sat apart from Buddha. His father explained that during Buddha's seven-year absence, Yashodhara had emulated everything Buddha did—she cut off her hair, gave up luxury, and ate from a simple clay bowl. This demonstrated her deep devotion. Buddha praised Yashodhara for her strength, loyalty, and bravery during his spiritual journey. He admired how nobly she had handled her grief and what a fine young boy Rahula had become. Then Buddha left the palace to continue his alms round.

Yashodhara dressed their seven-year-old son Rahula like a prince and told him to ask Buddha for his rightful inheritance. When Rahula asked which man was his father, she pointed to Buddha, who was eating with the other monks. Rahula approached Buddha with love and said, "Aren't you my father?

Holy one, even being near you brings joy! As your son, what inheritance do I receive?"

The Blessed One spoke earnestly, "Instead of perishable treasures that bring sorrow, I will give you the lasting inheritance of a holy life. I have no gold, silver, or jewels to offer—but I can give you something far more precious: spiritual wisdom. If you are ready to receive and preserve these teachings, I have abundance to share. My true treasure lies in teaching others how to live a good and righteous life. Would you like to join our community of monks who devote themselves to developing their minds and seeking genuine happiness?"

Rahula answered firmly, "Yes, I would."

When Suddhodana, Rahula's grandfather, heard that his grandson had become a monk, he was deeply saddened.

Last attempt to make Buddha a king Grieving at the thought of losing his son and grandson forever, Suddhodana asked his counselor and family priest to convince Buddha to return. Following the king's wishes, they caught up with Buddha on his journey, paid their respects, and sat with him beneath a tree where the family priest began to speak.

"O prince, consider for a moment the feelings of the king, whose eyes rain tears as the arrow of your departure pierces his heart. He has asked you to return home, saying only then can he die peacefully.

"I know your resolve is fixed upon religion, and I am convinced this purpose of yours is unchanging; yet I am consumed by anguish like a flame at your choice of this homeless state.

"Come, you who love duty—abandon this purpose for duty's sake—toward your family, your kingdom, and your people.

"Enjoy for a while the sovereignty of the earth—you shall go to the forest at the time prescribed by the sastras. Do not disregard your unhappy kindred. Compassion for all creatures is the true religion.

"Religion is not found only in forests. The salvation of ascetics can be accomplished even in a city. Thought and effort are the true means—the forest and its tokens are merely a coward's signs.

"The king of the Sakyas drowns in a deep sea of sorrow, full of waves of trouble springing from you. Deliver him, who is as helpless as an ox drowning in the sea.

"Consider also the queen who raised you, who has not yet gone to Agastya's realm—will you not heed her, who grieves ceaselessly like a cow that has lost her calf?

"Surely you will comfort your wife with your presence. She mourns as a widow though her lord still lives—like a swan separated from her mate or a female elephant deserted in the forest by her companion."

The Lord, having heard the words of the family priest, reflected for a moment and uttered his gentle reply:

"I well know the paternal tenderness of the king, which he has shown toward me. Yet knowing this, I am still alarmed at the ill and sorrow that pervades the world, and am inevitably forced to leave my kindred.

"Who would not wish to see their dear ones, if only separation did not exist? But since parting comes again even after reunion, it is for this reason I must abandon my father, however loving he may be.

"I cannot agree that you should think the king's grief is caused by me. Even in the midst of his dream-like unions, he is afflicted by thoughts of future separations.

"Let your thoughts settle into certainty, having seen the many forms of existence. Neither son nor kindred is the cause of sorrow—this sorrow is caused only by ignorance.

"Since parting is inevitably fixed in the course of time for all beings, just as for travelers who have joined company on a road—what wise person would cherish sorrow when losing their kindred, even though they love them?

"Leaving his kindred in another world, one departs here, and having left them here, goes forth once more. Having gone there, he goes elsewhere also—such is the lot of mankind. What attachment can the liberated have for them?

"Since death is inherent from the moment of birth, why, in your affection for your son, have you called my departure to the forest ill-timed?

"There may be an 'ill time' in attaining worldly objects—time indeed is inseparably connected with all things. Time draws the world through all its seasons, but any time suits a bliss that is truly worthy of praise.

"That the king should wish to surrender his kingdom to me is a noble thought, well worthy of a father. But it would be as improper for me to accept it as for a sick man through greed to accept unwholesome food.

"How can it be right for the wise to enter royalty, the home of illusion, where anxiety, passion, and weariness dwell, and where all right is violated through service to others?

"The golden palace seems to me to be on fire; the finest delicacies appear mixed with poison; the tranquil lotus-bed is infested with crocodiles."

Having heard the Buddha's discourse—which was well-suited to his virtues and knowledge, free from desires, full of sound reasoning, and profound—the counselor replied:

"This resolve of yours shows excellent judgment, not wrong in itself but only wrong for the present time. It cannot be your duty, loving duty as you do, to leave your father to sorrow in his old age.

"Surely your mind is not very discerning, or it fails to properly weigh duty, wealth, and pleasure—when you depart for an unseen result while disregarding what lies before you.

"Some say there is another birth, while others firmly claim there is not. Since the matter remains in doubt, it is wise to enjoy the good fortune that comes to hand.

"If there is life hereafter, we shall enjoy it as it comes. If there is no life beyond this one, then all beings are already assured liberation without effort.

"Some believe in a future life but deny the possibility of liberation. As fire is naturally hot and water naturally liquid, they hold that our actions are bound by their inherent nature.

"Some maintain that all things—good and evil, existence and non-existence—arise from inherent properties. Since the world arises spontaneously, they say our efforts are meaningless.

"Since our senses operate in fixed ways, and external objects are inherently pleasant or unpleasant—for a life bound to old age and pain, what effort can change its course? Does it not all unfold on its own?

"Fire is quenched by water, and fire causes water to evaporate; different elements, united in a body and producing unity, sustain the world.

"The wise declare that an embryo in the womb—composed of hands, feet, belly, back, and head, united with the soul—forms itself spontaneously.

"Who gives thorns their sharpness? Who determines the various natures of beasts and birds? All this arises spontaneously. If there is no action from desire, how can there be will?

"Others say creation comes from Brahma—what need then is there for the conscious soul's effort? That which causes the world's action also determines its cessation.

"Some say both the creation and destruction of being are caused by the soul, yet they claim creation requires no effort while liberation demands it.

"A man has three debts: to ancestors through offspring, to saints through sacred knowledge, and to gods through sacrifices. He is born with these debts—only by discharging them can he find liberation.

"Through these rules, the wise promise liberation to those who make effort. Yet even with all their energy, those seeking liberation will find weariness.

"Therefore, gentle youth, if you desire liberation, follow the prescribed path correctly. Thus you shall attain it, and the king's grief will end.

"As for your thoughts on life's evils leading you from forest to home—do not let this trouble you, my son. Many in ancient times have returned from forests to their houses."

The Buddhas firm refusal

Then, having heard the affectionate and loyal words of the minister, the Buddha—firm in his resolve—made his answer, with nothing omitted or displaced, neither tedious nor hasty: "This doubt whether anything exists or not cannot be solved for me by another's words. Having determined the truth through asceticism or quietism, I will myself grasp whatever truth there may be. "I cannot accept a theory that depends on the unknown, is poorly contested, and involves countless presuppositions. What wise man would go by another's belief?

Mankind is like the blind directed in darkness by the blind. "But even though I cannot discern the truth, if good and evil are in doubt, let one's mind be set on the good. Even a toil in vain is worthy of one whose soul is good.

"Having seen that this 'sacred tradition' is uncertain, know that only what has been uttered by the trustworthy is right. And know that trustworthiness means the absence of faults—he who is without faults will not utter an untruth. "

As for what you said about my returning home, the examples you give hold no authority—for in determining duty, how can you quote as authorities those who have broken their vows? "Even the sun may fall to earth, even Mount Himavat may lose its firmness, but never could I return to my home as a worldly man, with my senses merely alert for external objects. "I would enter the blazing fire, but not my house with my purpose unfulfilled."

Rising up in accordance with his resolve, full of detachment, he went his way. Then the minister, full of tears, having heard his firm determination and having followed him awhile with despondent looks, overcome with sorrow, slowly returned to Kapilavatsu.

They could neither behold him on the road nor lose sight of him—shining in his own splendor and beyond the reach of all others, like the sun. Having failed to persuade him to return home, the minister and the priest went back with faltering steps, saying to each other, "How shall we approach the king and see him, who is longing for his dear son?"

Chapter 13

The Order Of Bhikkus

When Buddha returned to his homeland, he found his people, the Sakyas, were divided into two groups. Some supported him while others opposed him. This situation brought back memories of earlier conflicts among the Sakyas during the Sakya-Koliya war.

Those who supported Buddha made an important decision—each family would send one son to follow and learn from him. These sons became his disciples and went with him to the city of Rajagraha.

One of these families was led by Amitodana. His son Mahanama gave his brother Anuruddha a choice: either Anuruddha would leave home to follow Buddha, or Mahanama would do it. Anuruddha, who had grown up in luxury, at first said he couldn't live as a homeless monk.

Mahanama continued, "But come now, dear Anuruddha, I will tell you what household life entails. First, you must have your fields ploughed, then sown. Next, you must irrigate them, then drain them. After that, you must pull up the seedlings, reap the crop, and carry it away. Then you must bundle it, thresh it, separate the straw, remove the chaff, and winnow the grain. Finally, you must store the harvest. And when all this is done, you must begin the same cycle again next year, and the year after that.

The work never ends; there is no final day of labor. When will our work be complete? When will we see the end of our toils? Can we really enjoy the pleasures of our five senses while dwelling in peace? No, dear Anuruddha, the work is never finished; it's an endless round of being tied to samsaric existence, going in circles like an ox tied to a pole. Our labors, when directed outward toward gaining material wealth just to satisfy our five senses, are endless. The Buddha teaches us to look inward and cultivate the garden within ourselves and be free from this endless cycle of samsaric existence. It would be a privilege to become a monk and learn from him."

"I'll become a monk then, and you can take care of the household," Anuruddha decided.

Anuruddha asked his mother three times for permission to leave home and become a monk. Though initially reluctant, she finally said yes, but with one condition—he could only go if his friend Bhaddiya went with him. At first, Bhaddiya didn't want to go, but he eventually agreed after asking for seven days to prepare.

Before they left to join Buddha, their family barber Upali shaved their heads. Anuruddha and Bhaddiya gave Upali their jewelry and ornaments, then set off on their journey.

Anuruddha was one of the foremost and famous disciples of Buddha who contributed to the spread of Buddhism far and wide after the passing away of Siddhartha.

Upali was worried that other Sakyan nobles might hurt him because of having jewelry, so he left it on a tree and decided to follow Anuruddha instead. When Anuruddha and Bhaddiya saw him, they thought this was a good idea. They knew their own people could be harsh. They brought Upali to Buddha and made an unusual request—they asked if Upali could join the Buddhist order before them. This was their way of becoming more humble, as they would need to show respect to someone who used to be their barber. Buddha agreed to their request. He accepted Upali first, and then welcomed the Sakyan nobles afterward.

There was also a man named Sunita who lived in the city of Rajagraha. He was from a low caste and worked as a street sweeper, collecting garbage for a living. One day, while Buddha was walking with his monks to collect food offerings, Sunita was cleaning the streets. When he saw Buddha approaching, he felt both happy and nervous. Out of respect, he pressed himself against a wall to make way. Buddha came up to him and kindly asked, "Sunita, why do you live like this? Would you like to join our community?" Sunita, filled with joy, asked to join the Order. The Master welcomed him, saying "Come, Bhikkhu!" and provided him robes. He taught Sunita the Dhamma, saying that holiness comes through discipline and self-mastery. When asked about Sunita's transformation, Buddha compared him to a lily growing from a rubbish heap of a divided —showing how wisdom can bloom anywhere.

A young boy named Sopaka, who was from a low-status family and had nearly died at birth, was raised by a cemetery caretaker along with the caretaker's son Suppiya. With his foster father's blessing, Sopaka joined Buddha's community. Later, Suppiya followed his friend's example and also became a monk, showing that social status didn't matter in Buddha's community.

Buddha welcomed people from all backgrounds into his community. He accepted farmers like Sumangala, former slaves like Channa, craftsmen like Dhanniya the potter, and humble workers like Kappata-Kura who sold grass. He treated everyone equally, no matter where they came from or what work they did.

One day in the city of Rajagraha, Buddha met a man named Supprabuddha who had leprosy and was looking for food. Buddha saw that this man was ready to learn, so he taught him about generosity, living a good life, and letting go of wants and desires. Buddha then shared his teaching about the Four Noble Truths. Supprabuddha was very open to learning, like a clean cloth ready for dye. As he listened to Buddha, he had a deep realization: he understood that everything that begins must also end. This simple but profound truth helped him fully understand Buddha's teachings. His doubts vanished, and he felt sure about what he had learned. Happy with his new understanding, Supprabuddha became a Bhikku.

It's impossible for us in modern times to recognize how revolutionary all of this was. In a chaturvarna society which was dominantly ruled by class and caste differences, where even accidentally looking at a higher class member by a lower class member entailed whipping and other punishments for the lower class, Buddha admitted everyone as equal into his sangha. Buddha emphasized only compassion and saw everyone as fellow human beings beyond their caste differences.

Admission of women into the Bhikkuni order

When Buddha visited their hometown, Mahaprajapati Gotami and other Sakya women requested to join the Sangha, but the Buddha initially refused. Despite their determination—shown by shaving their heads and traveling to Vesali—he maintained his refusal.

Ananda intervened on Gotami's behalf, reminding the Buddha that he could not refuse his teachings to his own stepmother who had raised him with loving care after his mother's death. When the Buddha refused again, Ananda challenged his decision. "My Lord, do you also share the prevailing Brahmin belief that women cannot reach moksha due to being inferior to men? You have allowed Shudras to join the Sangha—why treat women differently?"

The Buddha replied: "Ananda, do not misunderstand me. I hold that women are as capable as men of reaching Nibbana. I do not uphold the doctrine of sex inequality. My rejection of Mahaprajapati's request is based on safety reasons and practical grounds alone."

"I am glad to know the true reason, Lord. But should practical difficulties prevent you from granting her request? Would such a refusal not discredit the Dhamma as just another doctrine which supports inequality and invite accusations of gender discrimination? Could we not establish rules to address these practical concerns and ensure the safety of our brave women?"

"Well, Ananda, I will grant Mahaprajapati's request if she insists that women must be allowed to take Parivraja under my doctrine and discipline. However, it shall be subject to eight conditions (Garudhammas)" *(These 8 Garudhammas are disputed by modern scholars if they were really told by the Buddha) (1) Nuns and monks must show mutual respect through greetings and gestures (2) Nuns must reside in areas where monks are present during the rainy season retreat (3) Nuns must seek guidance from senior monks and nuns twice monthly on observance days and teachings (4) After the rainy season, nuns must report their observations to both orders (5) Nuns who break rules must undergo two weeks of meditative discipline before both orders (6) Probationer nuns must complete two years of training before seeking full ordination (7) Nuns must not abuse or disrespect monks or fellow nuns (8) Nuns must not admonish monks or fellow nuns*

Ananda returned and informed the Buddha that Mahaprajapati had accepted the Eight Chief Rules, thus receiving her Upasampada initiation into the Sangha. Mahaprajapati and 500 Sakya women were then ordained and received teachings directly from the Buddha. Among these new Bhikkhunis was Yashodhara, who became known as *Bhadda Kacchana.*

Admission of the fallen

In Rajagaha lived a robber named Angulimala who terrorized Kosala. He had neglected his parents and superiors, seeking merit through sun and moon worship while wearing a necklace made from his victims' fingers. Buddha sought him out despite warnings from villagers that he was beyond redemption. When they met, Angulimala came running toward the Buddha to attack him. Though swift and strong, Angulimala couldn't catch up to Buddha, which amazed him and led him to ask about Buddha's ways.

"I have stopped, Angulimala, for your sake. Will you stop following your career as an evildoer? I have been pursuing you to win you over, to convert you to the path of righteousness. The good in you is not yet dead. If you will only give it a chance, it will transform you."

Angulimala felt overcome by the words of the Blessed One, saying, "At last this sage has tracked me down, And now that thy hallowed words ask me to renounce evil deeds forever, I am prepared to give myself a trial," replied Angulimala.

Angulimala threw his necklace of victims' fingers into a deep abyss, fell at the Master's feet, and begged to join the Brotherhood. Buddha's words had touched his heart, leading to his transformation. After three years of fruitless offerings, he sought Buddha's guidance. The Lord explained the futility of sacrifice without inner transformation. The Buddha shared these teachings: "The enlightened one lives free from desire, dwelling in wisdom's light. The wise seek not worldly gains but follow the path of supreme understanding. Knowing life's impermanence, they guide others from impurity to virtue."

The King of Kosala was amazed to find the former robber had become one of Buddha's peaceful followers. At first, the king was afraid to meet him, but upon seeing Angulimala's transformation, he offered food and supplies. Angulimala declined these offers, choosing instead to live simply. Though local villagers, still angry about his past crimes, acted violently toward him, Angulimala remained calm and committed to his new peaceful way of life.

Importance of stepwise Training

One day at East Park in Shravasti, a man named Moggallana came to visit Buddha. After they greeted each other, Moggallana asked Buddha how he taught his students. "Teacher," Moggallana said, "we Brahmins teach our students step by step, like someone climbing stairs. Do you teach your students in a similar way?"

"Yes," Buddha replied. "Just like a good horse trainer starts with the basics before moving to advanced lessons, I also teach my students gradually, beginning with the simplest teachings."

"Come, brother, I will teach you! Be virtuous. Live within the restraints of our discipline. Master right behavior—seeing danger even in small faults—and learn the moral precepts. Once you have mastered these, I will teach you the second lesson: When seeing objects with your eyes, do not be captivated by their appearances or details.

"Guard against the misery that comes from uncontrolled visual cravings—these harmful states can overwhelm you like a flood. Master control over your sense of sight. Apply this same principle to all your senses. Whether hearing sounds, smelling scents, tasting flavors, touching objects, or thinking thoughts —do not let their surface features or details enchant you.

"After mastering this, the next lesson is: Be moderate in eating. Take your food mindfully and purposefully—not for pleasure or vanity, but to sustain the body, protect it from harm, and support your spiritual practice. Consider: 'I will restrain my old habits and avoid new cravings to maintain health and peace.'

"Once you have learned restraint in eating, the next lesson is: Dedicate yourself to watchfulness. During daylight hours, whether walking or sitting, purify your heart of hindrances. In the first watch of night, continue this practice. In the second watch, rest mindfully like a lion—on your right side, one foot upon the other. In the final watch, rise and resume purifying the heart through walking or sitting meditation.

"After becoming devoted to watchfulness, cultivate mindfulness and self-control. In every action—whether going forth or returning, looking around, bending or stretching, wearing robes, carrying bowls, eating, drinking, walking, standing, sitting, sleeping, waking, speaking, or keeping silent—maintain complete awareness and control.

"When self-control is established, seek solitude—in forests, at the foot of trees, on mountains, in caves or grottos, in charnel grounds, in forest retreats, in the open air, or on beds of straw. After your meal, sit cross-legged, maintain an upright posture, and practice the four stages of meditation.

"This, Moggallana, is how I train all disciples who are still learning, who have not yet mastered their minds, but who aspire to progress on the path. For enlightened arhants who have achieved liberation and self-control, these practices bring peace and mindfulness".

Moggallana asked Buddha whether all disciples reach Nibbana. Buddha explained that some do while others don't. When asked why, Buddha offered an analogy: Just as someone who knows the way to Rajagaha can guide others, yet some may still take wrong turns while others reach their destination, the Buddha merely shows the path—he cannot guarantee salvation.

Unlike prophets who promise divine salvation, Buddha's path emphasizes controlling one's passions to reach Nibbana. He acts as a guide, but each person must walk the path for themselves. Impressed by his teachings, Moggallana became a bhikkhu and joined Buddha's Order.

Chapter 14

What Is BuddhaDhamma?

Though the Buddha spread his teachings widely and gathered many dedicated followers, he claimed no special place for himself in his own Dhamma. He did not promise salvation, describing himself as ***Marga Data (Way Finder)*** rather than ***Moksha Data (Giver of Salvation)***. He claimed no divinity for himself or his teachings—

The Dhamma was discovered by humans, for humans, and was not a divine revelation.

Unlike other religious leaders who claimed divine status, the Buddha presented himself simply as the son of Suddhodana and Mahamaya, making no special claims about himself or requiring belief in him for salvation.

This humility was reflected in the first Buddhist congregation after his death at Rajagraha. Under Kassyappa's leadership, the focus was solely on preserving the Dhamma and Vinaya teachings. No effort was made to document Buddha's life story, demonstrating how he deliberately kept himself separate from his teachings. The Buddha maintained this clear distinction through his consistent refusal to appoint a successor, despite multiple requests from his followers.

His response was unequivocal: "The Dhamma must be its own successor. Principle must live by itself, not by the authority of man. If principle needs the authority of man, it is no principle. If one must invoke the founder's name to enforce the Dhamma's authority, then it is no Dhamma."

Unlike most religions, which are based on divine revelation and promises of salvation, Buddhism emerged through progressive human discovery, discourse with people, and investigation. Revealed religions typically present themselves as messages from God to humanity, delivered through prophets who promise salvation to their followers—usually meaning the saving of souls from damnation, conditional on dogmatically obeying divine commands and accepting the prophet's authority without question. The Buddha explicitly rejected this dogmatic role. Instead, he insisted everything must be subjected to rigorous examination.

His teaching was a progressive iterated discovery—the result of careful inquiry into human life, instincts, and the patterns of behavior shaped by history and tradition that often work against human wellbeing. While other religious leaders promised salvation, the Buddha stood apart as a teacher who made no such promise. As Marga Data, he emphasized that each person must seek their own salvation through personal effort.

The Buddha taught for forty years in various parts of the country, traveling by foot with his followers. He organized his teachings into three categories: Dhamma (teachings),

Adhamma (not-Dhamma), and Saddhamma (philosophy of Dhamma). Understanding all three is essential to grasp his complete teachings.

Maintaining purity of life is Dhamma. Reaching perfection in life is Dhamma. Living in Nibbana is Dhamma. Giving up craving is Dhamma. Understanding that all compound things are impermanent is Dhamma. Recognizing that present actions (karma) are the instruments of moral order is Dhamma.

To Maintain Purity of Life is Dhamma

The Buddha taught three forms of purity:

Purity of body means abstaining from killing, stealing, and harmful sensual acts.

Purity of speech means abstaining from falsehood and idle talk.

Purity of mind means being mindful of and abandoning unwholesome mental states—desire, hatred, sloth, agitation, and doubt.

One who achieves these three purities is considered "pure and unblemished."

Five obstacles that hinder training: 1. Taking life 2. Taking what is not given 3. Engaging in sensual misconduct 4. Speaking falsely 5. Using intoxicants

After overcoming these obstacles, one should practice the **four foundations of mindfulness**: 1. Contemplating the body 2. Contemplating feelings 3. Contemplating mind 4.

Contemplating Compassionate Ideas towards all beings (Maitreyi) Through diligent mindful observation, one develops self-mastery and overcomes discontent.

There are three types of failure:

Failure in morality includes taking life, stealing, misconduct, lying, and harmful speech.

Failure in mind manifests as covetousness and ill will.

Failure in view means denying the value of giving, rejecting the law of cause and effect, and believing only in the material world.

The three successes are:

Success in morality: Abstaining from harmful actions and speech

Success in mind: Freedom from greed and ill will

Success in view: Understanding the merit of giving, the power of actions, and the existence of both material and spiritual realms.

These successes lead to Nirvana & The cessation of suffering

To Reach Perfection in Life is Dhamma

(It was explained in a discourse to a Bhikkuni called Shubuti)

Through the destruction of defilements (asavas), one achieves liberation in this very life—gaining complete understanding of both the heart's release and the release through insight, free from all defilements. Having reached this state, one dwells within it. This is called "***perfection in mind.***"

A Bodhisattva's ***perfection of giving*** emerges when they offer both internal and external gifts with complete understanding. They share these gifts with all beings and dedicate them to supreme enlightenment, inspiring others to do the same—while remaining free from attachment.

A Bodhisattva's ***perfection of morality*** means living virtuously while guiding others to do likewise.

A Bodhisattva's ***perfection of patience*** means embodying patience while helping others develop it.

A Bodhisattva's ***perfection of vigor*** means maintaining dedication to the unwavering vigorous effort to the task while supporting others on this path. A

Bodhisattva's ***perfection of concentration*** means mastering meditation without clinging to heavenly realms, while teaching others to do the same.

A Bodhisattva's ***perfection of wisdom*** means remaining unattached to any dharma while understanding the true nature of all dharmas, and helping others gain this understanding. It is Dhamma to cultivate these perfections.

The Buddha explains the "law of practice" here. We become good at what we do by practicing repeatedly and teaching others.

To Live in Nibbana is Dhamma

(Discourse with the Bhikkhus of Gaya)

Nibbana simply means ***"the liberation from suffering."*** "Nothing can give real happiness like Nibbana," said the

Buddha. Of all his doctrines, the teaching of Nibbana is the most central.

What is Nibbana? Before Buddha taught about it, other teachers had different ideas about what it meant. They thought of Nibbana in three main ways:

1. *The materialistic view (Laukik):* This focused on excessive hedonistic physical pleasures—eating, drinking, sensual activities, and enjoying life—as the way out of suffering.

2. *The Yogic view:* This was about meditation and withdrawing from the world as the way out of suffering.

3. The Brahmanic view: This focused on saving the soul through worship, prayers, and animal sacrifices, while asking another supernatural entity to be our savior from suffering.

Buddha disagreed with all these ideas. He rejected the Brahmanic views because they believed in a permanent soul and denied human autonomy and free will. He also disagreed with the materialistic view because it only focused on physical pleasures. Buddha explained that constantly chasing pleasures doesn't bring real happiness—it actually leads to more unhappiness.

As for the Yogic approach, Buddha saw it as incomplete. While meditation could bring temporary peace by avoiding life's problems, this peace didn't last. It only worked while someone was meditating, and then the problems would return. We cannot meditate all day just to avoid mental suffering.

The Buddha's conception of Nibbana differed significantly from all these predecessors. Three key ideas underpin his view:

First, it concerns the happiness of sentient beings, rather than the salvation of a soul.

Second, it focuses on the happiness of sentient beings in Samsara during their lifetime. The notion of a soul and its salvation after death are completely foreign to the Buddha's conception of Nibbana.

Third, it emphasizes controlling the ever-burning flames of passion.

The Fire Sermon

In a sermon given at Gaya, Buddha used a powerful metaphor to explain human suffering. He compared our inner struggles to fire, saying "Everything we experience is burning." He explained: "Our eyes and everything we see are burning. Our awareness of what we see is burning. Even the feelings we get from seeing things—whether good, bad, or neutral—are all burning."

"What makes them burn?" his followers asked.

"They burn with passion, hatred, and confusion," Buddha answered. "They burn with the pain of birth, aging, death, sadness, grief, and despair." He continued: "This is true for all our senses—our ears and what we hear, our nose and what we smell, our tongue and what we taste, our body and what we feel, our mind and what we think. All these experiences and their resulting feelings are burning."

"And what fuels this fire?" they asked again.

"The same forces," Buddha replied. "Passion, hatred, and confusion. The suffering of birth, aging, death, sadness, grief, and despair." Buddha concluded with hope: "When wise people understand this truth, they naturally begin to let go of these burning passions. As they release them, they become free from passion's grip. When they're free, they know their freedom."

Many believe that unhappiness comes from not having material things, yet this isn't true. Even those surrounded by the world's riches can be unhappy. Unhappiness springs from uncontrolled fiery passions: "Excited by greed (lobha), furious with anger (dosa), blinded by delusion (moha), with mind overwhelmed and enslaved, people dwell on their own misfortunes and those of others, experiencing mental suffering and anguish. If, however, greed, anger, and delusion are overcome, people no longer dwell on misfortune or experience mental suffering and anguish."

"Thus, brothers, is Nibbana visible in this life and not merely in the future—inviting, attractive, accessible to the wise disciple who subdues lobha, dosa, and moha."

The Buddha's metaphor of burning fire illuminates the cause of human suffering. Our passions—like a consuming fire—are the source of unhappiness. These passions act as fetters, blocking the path to Nibbana. Only by freeing oneself from these passions can one achieve happiness through Nibbana.

According to Buddha's teachings, three main types of passions cause our suffering:

1. Craving and attachment (lobha) - This includes desires, greed, and excessive attachment to things or people

2. Negative feelings (dosa) - This includes hatred, anger, and all forms of aversion toward others

3. Ignorance (moha or avidya) - This means not understanding the truth, being confused, or lacking wisdom

The first two types concern our emotions and relationships with others. The third type relates to our understanding (or misunderstanding) of reality.

Some misinterpret what Buddha meant by "Nibbana." The word means "to blow out" or "to extinguish," which has led to confusion. Critics wrongly claim that Nibbana means the death of all feelings and passions—essentially, a kind of death itself. This is incorrect. The Fire Sermon helps us understand Buddha's true meaning. The sermon doesn't say life itself needs to be extinguished—it says our harmful passions are like a fire that causes suffering. Importantly, Buddha didn't teach that we must eliminate all passions. Instead, he taught us not to feed these fires by adding more fuel to them.

Isn't a life without passions like death (Parinibbana)? Did Buddha teach this? Another common misconception is the confusion between Nibbana and Parinibbana. Parinibbana occurs at death—when the body dies, consciousness ends, and all feelings and sensations cease completely. It marks a final ending. But Nibbana is fundamentally different. It means having sufficient self-control over our emotions and desires to live a good, moral life.

Buddha made clear that Nibbana isn't about ending everything—it's about living righteously following the Middle Path, everything in moderation. He explained this directly to his student Radha:

"Pray Lord, what is Nibbana?"

"Nibbana means release from passion. Rooted in Nibbana, Radha, the righteous life is lived. Nibbana is its goal. Nibbana is its end."

The virtuous life following Madhyama Marga is its own reward. That Nibbana does not mean complete extinction of passions is further clarified by Sariputta in this sermon:

"Brethren, know that greed is vile, and vile is resentment. To shed this greed and resentment, there is the Middle Way which gives us eyes to see and makes us know, leading us to peace, insight, enlightenment, and Nibbana.

"What is this Middle Way? It is nothing but the Noble Eightfold Path of right outlook, right aims, right speech, right action, right means of livelihood, right effort, right mindfulness, and right concentration—this, brethren, is the Middle Way.

"Indeed, anger is vile and malevolence is vile, envy and jealousy are vile, niggardliness and avarice are vile, hypocrisy and deceit and arrogance are vile, inflation is vile, and indolence is vile.

"For the shedding of anger, malevolence, pride, jealousy, avarice, inflation, and indolence, there is the Middle Way—giving us eyes to see, making us know, and leading us to peace, insight, and enlightenment." The idea underlying Nibbana is that it is the path of righteousness. None shall mistake Nibbana for anything else.

Complete surrender to hedonistic inflaming passions is one extreme, and complete extinction of passions (Parinibbana) is another extreme. Nibbana is the Middle Way.

To Give up Craving is Dhamma

In the Dhammapada, the Buddha says: "There is no greater benefit than health, and there is nothing more valuable than the spirit of contentment." This spirit of contentment should not be mistaken for passive acceptance or meek nihilistic surrender to circumstances, as this would contradict the Buddha's other teachings.

The Buddha never proclaimed "Blessed are they who are poor," nor did he suggest any inherent virtue in poverty. On the contrary, he recognized poverty as a root cause of human suffering. Rather than accepting their condition, he taught sufferers to practice Virya—energetic action. Material wealth is necessary to alleviate the suffering of those in dire poverty and hunger. Wealth itself was welcome in his view, provided one didn't cling to it with passion or greed. The key was to avoid both extremes: neither poverty nor obsession with wealth. This reflects the Madhyama Marga (the middle path). When the Buddha declared contentment to be the highest form of wealth, he meant we should not let ourselves be controlled by endless greed.

Rathapala described greed's grip on power: "Kings amass wealth without sharing, forever chasing more. Even vast kingdoms aren't enough—both rulers and subjects die wanting more."

Buddha explained to Ananda how greed grows: First comes wanting, Want grows into desire, Desire becomes attachment, Finally, attachment turns to greed. Greed leads to endless suffering.

Buddha warned that greed requires vigilant attention due to its dangers. It breeds conflict between people—leading to fighting, arguments, lies, and slander. This illustrates how greed sows discord among different groups. That's why Buddha emphasized the importance of mastering our wants and desires.

To believe that all things are impermanent is Dhamma

The Buddhist teaching of impermanence focuses on three main ideas: how composite things are finite, how living beings undergo constant change, and how dependent things are temporary.

As Buddhist philosopher Asanga explains, all things arise from combinations of causes and conditions, with no independent existence. When these combinations break apart, the thing ceases to exist.

For example, a living body combines earth, water, fire, and air elements—when these separate, the body dissolves. Impermanence of the living individual is best described by the formula—**Being Is Becoming**. A being in the past moment has lived, but does not live now nor will live in the future. A being in a future moment will live but has neither lived before nor lives now. A being in the present moment lives now but has not lived before and will not live in the future. In essence, a human being is constantly changing and growing, never remaining the same from one moment to the next.

While it's easy to grasp that all living beings will eventually die, it's more challenging to understand how a human being continuously changes—or "becomes"—while alive. You're not the same person as yesterday. "How is this possible?" The Buddha's answer was simple: "This is possible because all is impermanent." This concept later gave rise to what is called **Śūnya Vāda.**

Buddhist Śūnyatā doesn't mean nothingness or negativism—it refers to the perpetual changes occurring at every moment in the phenomenal world.

Like a river flowing continuously, you cannot step into the same river twice.

The river you stepped into yesterday doesn't exist now. It keeps flowing—the water that touched you yesterday has passed, because of its impermanence. Precisely because of that impermanence, the river of today exists. Today's flowing river gives way to the river of tomorrow. It's the same with everything in the universe. *To be now is to become something new every moment.*

Few people realize that Śūnyatā isn't nihilistic. It's the most life-affirming philosophy ever propounded. Impermanence makes everything possible—without it, nothing in the world could exist. The possibility of all things existing depends on their impermanent nature. If things were permanent and unchangeable rather than constantly changing, the evolution of life and development of living beings would cease. If humans remained in the same state until death, progress would halt. This doctrine affirms life rather than promoting death, passivity, or nihilism.

"All things are impermanent" was the Buddha's doctrine. But what is the moral of this teaching?

The moral is beautifully simple: do not be cravingly attached to anything. The Buddha taught detachment—from property, from friends, from all things—because "All these are impermanent."

To believe that Present Action (Karma) shapes our future is Dhamma - The law of Cause & Effect

Everything in nature follows regular patterns that we can see in our daily lives: The stars and planets move in ways we can predict, The four seasons follow the same pattern year after year, Plants follow a simple cycle: seeds grow into plants, which make fruits containing new seeds. In Buddhism, we call these natural patterns "Niyamas." For example, the pattern of seasons is called "Rutu Niyam," and the pattern of plant growth is called "Bija Niyam." Just like these patterns exist in nature, there are also patterns in how people behave and treat each other. We call this "moral order." But this makes us wonder: What creates these rules for human behavior?

Many people say religion explains moral order. They believe God makes all the rules - both for nature and human behavior. Their simple answer is: God creates rules, and we should follow them because God made us. But this answer has problems. If God controls everything and makes all the rules, why do people still do bad things? Why doesn't everyone just follow God's rules?

Some people tried to fix these problems with a different explanation. They said that God first created everything and set up basic rules for how things work. Then God stepped back and let nature run on its own following these rules. In this view, when things go wrong, it's nature's fault, not God's. But this idea has problems too.

If God just sets things up and then steps away, why do we need God in the explanation at all? This idea of a hands-off God doesn't really solve our questions.

Buddha offered a distinct explanation for how moral order is maintained. He taught that karma (the law of cause and effect) — not any divine being — maintains moral order in the universe. The quality of this moral order, whether good or bad, depends entirely on human actions.

Karma (kamma) refers to our actions and their effects (vipaka). Good actions (kusala kamma) create a positive moral order in society, while harmful actions (akusala kamma) create a negative one. Buddha explained karma as a natural law — *every action has a consequence that follows as inevitably as night follows day*. Like any law of nature, good actions invariably lead to positive effects, and no one can escape the consequences of harmful actions. His message was straightforward: perform good actions to create a better world for everyone. Avoid harmful actions because they damage society and create problems for humanity.

In some cases, karma may not produce any effect. This occurs when: The action is too insignificant to create an effect or The action is neutralized by other, more powerful actions Importantly, karmic effects don't always return to the person who performed the action. *One person*'s *actions may affect others instead*. Regardless, these effects contribute to society's overall moral order.

While individual human actions are temporary, this system of moral cause and effect persists in maintaining universal order. This explains why Buddhism centers on morality rather than divine authority. The law of karma provides Buddha's elegant explanation for how moral order sustains itself. Yet many misinterpret its purpose — it's not about personal fortune but about ***how our collective actions weave the moral fabric of our world***.

In essence, the law of karma forms part of Dhamma (Buddha's teachings) because it reveals how our actions shape our universe's moral nature.

Chapter 15

What Is Not Dhamma (Adhamma)

These are the main beliefs and practices that go against Buddhist teachings (Dhamma): Believing in supernatural powers, Believing in the existence of a permanent soul, Performing religious animal sacrifices, Following beliefs based on guesswork rather than evidence, Just collecting knowledge without using it in daily life, Blindly accepting religious texts as perfect truth (including Buddha's own teachings)

Believing in supernatural powers

People naturally seek to understand why things happen. Sometimes the connection between cause and effect is clear —like touching a hot stove and getting burned. But other times, the cause isn't obvious because it occurred long ago or far away. When people can't explain events, they often attribute them to supernatural or magical forces. Buddha rejected this idea, teaching that everything has a natural cause—either from human actions or natural laws. Buddha challenged those who believed fate, time, nature, or gods controlled everything. He posed crucial questions: If these forces control everything, what role do humans play? Are we mere puppets? Why have free will and intelligence if we simply blame everything on supernatural forces?

Buddha's position was clear: Since humans have free will and the ability to make rational decisions based on truth, events must arise from either human actions or natural causes. Supernatural events don't exist. He acknowledged that sometimes we can't immediately understand why something happened. However, he believed that through careful investigation and our intelligence, we can discover the true causes.

Buddha rejected supernatural beliefs for three key reasons:

1. He wanted people to think rationally and logically

2. He wanted people to freely search for truth

3. He wanted to eliminate dogmatism and superstition, which prevents questioning and learning

This is why Buddha taught about karma (cause and effect) instead of supernatural powers. He believed worship of supernatural forces contradicts true Buddhist teachings (Dhamma).

People often ask "Who created the world?" Many answer that God created it. In traditional Indian beliefs, this creator God has different names like Prajapati, Ishwar, Brahma, or Maha Brahma. However, no one can explain where this God came from.

People who believe in God usually describe him as: All-powerful (Omnipotent), Present everywhere (Omnipresent), All-knowing (Omniscient), Perfectly Good, Completely Just, Loving to all

Did Buddha believe God created the universe? No. He had several reasons for rejecting God's existence:

1. No one has ever seen God—people only talk about God without direct evidence

2. The world wasn't created by God—it developed naturally over time through evolution

3. There's no practical benefit to believing in God

4. Buddha taught that basing a religion on God leads to guesswork rather than truth

To illustrate this, Buddha shared a conversation with two Brahmin scholars, Vasettha and Bhardvaja, who were debating the right path to reach God.

Vasettha argued that all religious paths eventually lead to God, just as different roads in a village lead to the town center. Buddha responded with a simple question: "Has any Brahmin scholar ever actually seen God face to face?" When Vasettha admitted no one had, Buddha offered two compelling analogies: First, he likened them to a line of blind people holding onto each other—none can see where they're going, yet they follow one another. Second, he asked Vasettha to imagine someone claiming to be in love with the most beautiful woman in the land—without ever having seen her. How could they know anything about her?

In his discussion with Bhardvaja and Vasettha about a creator god, Buddha presented several logical arguments. First, he examined how God viewed himself, noting that God claims to be "the Great Creator, the All-powerful, the Ruler of All, and the Father of everything that exists or will exist." Isn't that a little narcissistic and egotistical?

Second, Buddha identified a contradiction: "You say God is eternal and unchanging. Yet humans—supposedly created by God—are temporary and ever-changing. Why do we die? The presence of God doesn't explain impermanence." Vasettha couldn't respond.

Third, Buddha challenged the concept of divine omnipotence: "If God controls everything, humans would have no free will or reason to act. We'd be passive puppets. Everything would be determined from the beginning till the end of time. If everything is known, what's the reason for creation? Where is the place for possibilities? Why would God create beings with the ability to think and choose?" Again, Vasettha had no answer.

Fourth, Buddha raised the question about good and evil: "If God is completely good and created everything, why do people commit evil acts? Why do some become thieves, liars, and murderers? If evil exists, that means God isn't all good or all powerful. Wouldn't this actually mean God created evil?" This question went unanswered.

Fifth, Buddha questioned how God can be omniscient, just, and merciful simultaneously: "If God is just and merciful, what does God do with murderers? Does he remain merciful and pardon them, or provide justice to the affected by imprisoning them? Or going one step further: With unlimited power, why doesn't God reform the murderer instantly and bring the victim back to life? Why do lies often triumph over truth? This suggests God cannot be just."

Buddha highlighted another logical problem: "Let's say God has introduced evil into the world to test mankind's goodness and free will. The existence of evil causes life's fundamental suffering. Doesn't this mean God is spectating a cosmic joke? Or if you say everything is determined by God and if an all-powerful God controls everything—both good and bad—then God must be responsible for evil. Either humans lack free will, God isn't good, or God is unaware of what happens."

Buddha offered additional reasons for rejecting belief in God: First, he considered discussions about God's existence unhelpful. Instead, he believed religion should focus on human behavior and promoting universal happiness. Second, he opposed religious ceremonies and rituals, viewing them as sources of superstition that contradicted right understanding (Samma Ditthi), a fundamental aspect of his teachings. Third, he saw belief in God as dangerous because it encouraged excessive worship and prayer, giving priests too much power to spread superstition and inhibit clear thinking.

Buddha's strongest argument came from his teaching of ***Dependent Origination (Patit Samutpad).***

He posed a simple question: How did God create the world? According to Buddha, only two possibilities existed: Did God create something from nothing, or did God create something from existing materials? He explained that creating something from nothing is impossible. However, if God used existing materials, those materials must have preceded God's creation. Therefore, God could not be the original creator of everything. Through this reasoning, Buddha concluded that belief in a supernatural God as the universe's creator contradicts true Buddhist teachings (Dhamma), and he considered it a false belief.

Believing in the existence of a soul

Buddha had clear reasons for rejecting the concept of a soul. Here's what he taught: First, he argued that belief in a soul lacks empirical evidence & promotes unnecessary superstitions. While we can observe and study the mind's workings, no one has ever detected or communicated with a soul. The concept of a soul was—and remains—as widespread as belief in God. It held particular significance in the Brahmanic religion, where it was known as "Atma" or "Atman."

According to this belief, the soul: Resides within but remains separate from the body, Exists from birth, Is immortal and transmigrates between bodies, Uses the body as a temporary vessel. Buddha rejected these notions entirely.

His teaching of ***"An-atta"—meaning "no soul"***—challenged believers with fundamental questions: What is a soul's exact nature? What is its origin? What occurs after death? Where does it go? What is its form? What is its duration? To demonstrate the concept's vagueness, Buddha posed simple yet profound questions about a soul's physical properties, revealing how believers struggled to explain their own convictions.

To explain his rejection of bodies & souls as distinct entities, Buddha developed the Nama-Rupa theory. According to Buddha, every living being consists of two primary elements:

1. Physical elements (Rupa Khanda)—the basic constituents of our body, comprising the natural elements of earth, water, fire, and air

2. Mental elements (Nama Khanda)—our consciousness (Vignana), which encompasses three crucial aspects: Sensory feelings from worldly interactions **(Vedana)**, Thoughts, Perceptual and comprehension abilities **(Sanna)**, Mental states arising due to these feelings & thoughts **(Sankara)**

Put simply, Buddha viewed each person as an integrated system of body and mind working in harmony, rather than degrading the body to just as a vessel housing a separate noble soul. Buddha taught that consciousness and physical elements are interrelated, though not in a simple causal relationship. *(To explain this relationship, we use an analogy: Just as a magnetic field always accompanies an electric field without being caused by it)* Consciousness accompanies the physical body and could be viewed as an "induced field" in relation to physical form (Rupa-Kaya).

The presence of consciousness transforms physical matter into a living, thinking being. This makes consciousness essential to human existence.

Consciousness operates in three fundamental ways:

1. It enables understanding (cognitive): It provides insight into our internal experiences, It facilitates comprehension of our environment

2. It generates feelings (emotional): It produces pleasure and pain, It shapes our experiences

3. *It motivates action (volitional):* It generates purposeful aims, It creates motivation Consciousness underlies all human experience and action.

This led Buddha to a compelling question: If consciousness performs all these functions, what role remains for a soul? Since consciousness already accomplishes everything attributed to a soul, the concept becomes unnecessary. Through this reasoning, Buddha demonstrated why souls don't exist and why belief in them cannot be part of Buddhist teaching (Dhamma).

Performing religious animal sacrifices

In ancient times, people thought religious sacrifices were very important. They had two types: First were the "*Nittya*" sacrifices - these were religious duties everyone had to do as mandated by the Brahman priests, without expecting anything in return. Second were the "*Naimitik*" sacrifices - people did these when they wanted something specific, like more money or success. These ceremonies often involved drinking alcohol, killing animals, and celebrations. People considered these practices holy, even though they involved harm to animals.

Buddha didn't agree with sacrifices being part of religion. When One scholar named Kutadanta asked Buddha to explain why sacrifices weren't spiritually valuable. Buddha answered by telling a story:

"Once there was a rich king called Maha Vigeta. He had lots of gold, silver, and other treasures. His storehouses were full of valuable things and food." One day, while the king was thinking deeply about preserving his well being, he considered making a big sacrifice to the Gods. But his advisor had a better idea.

Instead of focussing on sacrifice, the advisor suggested using his wealth to helping people: give farmers seeds and food, give traders money to start businesses, and pay government workers fairly. The king followed this advice. Soon, there were fewer crimes, the kingdom made more money, and everyone lived peacefully. People felt so safe they didn't even lock their doors.

The advisor then helped the king plan a different kind of sacrifice. This new type of sacrifice was special - no animals were killed, no trees were cut down, and nobody was forced to participate. They only used pure offerings like butter, oil, milk, honey, and sugar. Buddha concluded, "Do your sacrifices like King Vigeta did. Killing animals is cruel and wrong. It won't help you reach heaven."

When asked if there was a better sacrifice, Buddha replied that following moral precepts was superior. He explained: "Sacrificing your internal vices of greed, Hatred, Ignorance is far superior. When a person with a trusting heart commits to these precepts—abstaining from destroying life, from taking what is not given, from lustful misconduct, from speaking lies, and from strong intoxicating drinks that lead to carelessness —this is a sacrifice better than open generosity, better than perpetual alms, better than giving shelter, and better than accepting guidance."

A good sacrifice has three simple requirements: 1. It should be done at the right time 2. It should not harm any living beings 3. It should be done with good intentions

Wise and spiritual people approve of these kinds of sacrifices. They especially support two types of offerings: 1. Religious gifts given with pure intentions 2. Simple acts of kindness and generosity Hearing this, Kutadanta praised Buddha's wisdom.

Following beliefs based on guesswork rather than evidence

Throughout history, people have always wondered about big questions about life. They mainly thought about two things: understanding themselves and figuring out how everything in the universe started.

When thinking about themselves, people asked questions like: Have I lived before?, What kind of being was I in past lives?, Will I continue to exist after I die?, What will happen to me then?

They also had questions about their current life: Am I real?, What exactly am I?, Where did I come from?, Where am I going? When it came to the universe, they asked simple but deep questions like: Who made everything? Will it go on forever?

People came up with many different answers. Some thought a god named Brahma made everything, while others believed it was a different god called Prajapati. Some people said the universe would last forever, others said it wouldn't. Some thought the universe had an end point, while others believed it went on forever.

Buddha declined to answer these speculative questions, explaining that only those who are misguided would dwell on such unknowable matters. He provided three clear reasons:

1. These questions are not essential to spiritual practice.

2. Answering them would require omniscience—which no one possesses. Buddha himself acknowledged that knowledge is always incomplete and continues to grow

3. These concepts are mere speculation without any way to verify or disprove them

Buddha emphasized that such questions arise purely from imagination, lacking any factual foundation. He posed a crucial question: "How do these theories benefit people in their everyday lives and relationships?" His straightforward conclusion was: ***They don't help at all.***

Just collecting knowledge without using it in daily life

While ancient scholars valued knowledge above all else, Buddha emphasized its practical application. He advocated for universal education but stressed that knowledge must serve a purpose. Buddha insisted that knowledge should be paired with virtue (Sila), warning that knowledge without moral guidance could be harmful.

To illustrate this principle, he shared the story of Patisena, which demonstrated how virtue surpassed mere learning (Prajna). In Sravasti lived an elderly monk named Patisena who struggled with learning. Despite receiving daily lessons from 500 advanced monks for three years, he couldn't memorize even one verse of Buddhist teachings.

When the community ridiculed him for his slow learning, Buddha, feeling compassion, called Patisena over and gently taught him a simple verse: "*The person who guards their speech, controls their thoughts, and harms no one through their actions will find freedom.*"

Moved by Buddha's kindness, Patisena opened his heart and finally remembered this one verse. Buddha then said, "You're an elderly man who knows just one verse, and others might still mock you. Let me explain its meaning—listen carefully." After understanding Buddha's teachings about right conduct, Patisena achieved enlightenment.

When 500 Buddhist nuns requested a teacher, Buddha chose Patisena. Doubting his wisdom because he knew only one verse, the nuns planned to embarrass him by reciting his teaching backwards. Upon arriving to teach, Patisena humbly acknowledged his limited learning. Yet when the nuns attempted to mock him, they found themselves unable to speak. Humbled, they listened as Patisena explained the verse's meaning, and through his teaching, all attained enlightenment.

The following day at King Prasenjit's palace, a guard denied Patisena entry, dismissing him as a simple monk who knew only one verse. Buddha personally escorted Patisena inside, revealing to the astonished gathering that this monk had achieved enlightenment. "How could someone who knows just one verse attain such wisdom?" asked the king.

Buddha replied, "You don't need vast knowledge. Right conduct comes first. Patisena truly grasped the profound meaning of that one verse. It transformed his thoughts, speech, and actions. What value is there in knowing many things if that knowledge neither improves your life nor helps you avoid harmful ways?" Buddha continued, "Memorizing a thousand verses without understanding is worth less than deeply comprehending and living by a single teaching. One truth fully embodied is the path to freedom. Mere recitation without understanding serves no purpose. True wisdom emerges from deeply understanding and living by even a single teaching." Upon hearing this, everyone present—the monks, the king, and his officials—experienced profound joy.

Blindly accepting religious texts (including Buddha's own teachings) as infallible isnt Dhamma

Long ago, religious scholars believed their religious texts were perfect and beyond questioning. Buddha disagreed with three key points: these texts weren't sacred, they weren't final, and they could contain mistakes.

While other philosophers of his time sided with the dogmatic religious scholars to gain popularity, Buddha remained true to his convictions. He compared these religious texts to an empty desert, saying they prevented people from questioning and discovering true wisdom.

Buddha encouraged people to question everything. During a visit to a group called the Kalamas, who were confused by conflicting teachings from different teachers, Buddha validated their confusion and offered straightforward guidance.

He said, "Don't believe something just because someone told you about it, it's an old tradition, everyone believes it, it's in holy books, it partially makes sense, it matches your existing beliefs, or an important person said it."

The Kalamas asked, "What should we do instead?"

Buddha offered them a simple test: "Ask yourself one question: Does the teaching help you and your fellow beings in the present moment? If it's helpful, follow it. If not, discard it—regardless of who advocates it."

He further advised them to examine whether teachings make people greedy, hateful, or violent; lead to dishonesty or harmful behavior; or cause people to hurt others. Above all, he emphasized considering whether something leads to suffering.

Through these practical questions, Buddha helped the Kalamas understand that harmful actions inevitably cause suffering. He taught them to evaluate ideas based on their outcomes rather than their sources.This practical approach to testing ideas remains valuable today.

Did this mean Buddha wanted everyone to become atheists? No. Accept religious teachings with a pinch of rationality. The middle way, again. As we will see in later sections, Buddha acknowledged religion's role in maintaining social coherence and function. However, he believed religion's purpose should be to promote human well-being in the present, emphasizing personal virtues over fear-mongering, abstract metaphysical questions, and rituals.

He didn't oppose religion itself—only dogmatic fundamentalism. This reflects the true essence of Buddhist teachings. Buddha firmly rejected the dogmatism of his era, teaching that everything should undergo careful examination. Any teaching that doesn't reduce individual or collective suffering and enhance human well-being should be rejected.

Chapter 16

Sadhamma - The true Purpose of Dhamma

To Cleanse the Mind of its Impurities

In Shravasti, Buddha taught to a crowd including two merchants - one who respected his teachings and one who mocked them. That night, the respectful merchant drank moderately while the mocker drank heavily and died on the road. The first merchant later became king of a distant land and invited Buddha to teach his people.

Upon arrival, Buddha explained how the two merchants' different choices led to their different fates: "The mind is the source of everything. What we think shapes who we are and what happens to us. If someone thinks harmful thoughts, their words and actions become harmful too. The suffering that follows is like a wheel following the ox that pulls it. But if someone thinks good thoughts, their words and actions become good too. The happiness that follows is like a shadow that never leaves them." After hearing this teaching, the king, his ministers, and many others became Buddha's followers.

To Make the World a Kingdom of Righteousness

What is religion's purpose? Different religions answer this question in distinct ways. Most commonly, religions exist to help people find God and achieve salvation.

Most religions describe three realms: 1. Heaven—ruled by God 2. Earth—where humans dwell; 3. Hell—ruled by evil.

Earth exists between heaven and hell. Neither good nor evil has complete dominion here, though many believe God will ultimately prevail on Earth.

Religions view heaven in two primary ways: (1) As a perfect earthly realm where God's goodness reigns supreme (2) As a transcendent realm attainable through faith and religious devotion, offering eternal rewards to the faithful.

Traditional religions emphasize reaching heaven as life's ultimate goal and focus their teachings on this pursuit. Buddha's perspective on religion's purpose stood apart. Rather than emphasizing heavenly rewards after death, he taught that we should create an ideal world in the present. He showed that ending suffering requires treating one another with kindness and fairness. Through these practices, we can transform our world into a realm of justice and goodness—this distinguished his teachings from other faiths.

Buddha established practical guidelines through the Eightfold Path (Ashtanga Marga), and the Virtues (Paramitas). These formed his teaching's foundation by showing people how to live ethically.

He taught that human suffering stems from our unjust treatment of each other. Living righteously—doing what is right and fair—is the only path to end this suffering. Thus, Buddha insisted that religion must go beyond mere preaching about God & help people deeply understand the importance of ethical behavior.

According to Buddha, any religion should serve these essential purposes: 1. Teaching and encouraging right action 2. Identifying and helping people avoid wrongdoing 3. Training people to develop positive habits and attitudes.

A virtuous disposition provides the only lasting foundation for genuine goodness. This explains Buddha's emphasis on mental training—cultivating one's disposition. He also stressed another vital element: *the courage to uphold what is right, even when nobody is watching us.*

In the Sallekha-Sutta, Buddha taught these principles:

"Though others may be harmful, resolve to be harmless.

Though others may kill, resolve never to kill.

Though others may steal, resolve not to steal.

Though others may abandon the higher life, resolve to pursue it.

Though others may lie, deceive, or spread rumors, resolve to speak truth.

Though others may be greedy, resolve to be content.

Though others may be malicious, resolve to be kind.

Though others may follow wrong views, aims, speech, actions, and concentration, resolve to follow the Noble Eightfold Path—

right outlook, aims, speech, actions, livelihood, effort, mindfulness, and concentration.

Though others may misunderstand truth and liberation, resolve to understand them correctly.

Though others may be lazy or dull, resolve to be energetic.

Though others may be arrogant, resolve to be humble.

Though others may be doubtful, resolve to be clear-minded.

Though others may harbor anger, spite, jealousy, greed, deceit, arrogance, bad company, carelessness, disbelief, shamelessness, and ignorance, resolve to cultivate their opposites.

Though others may cling to temporary things, resolve to embrace the timeless and practice renunciation."

"The development of will is essential for right consciousness, speech, and action. Therefore, you must develop the will to uphold all these resolutions."

This exemplifies Buddha's vision of religion's true purpose.

To Go Beyond Mere Pedantic Learning

The Brahminic doctrine restricted education to male members of the three upper classes, excluding women and Shudras from even basic literacy. The Buddha opposed this view, teaching that knowledge should be available to all. This led to a debate with Lohikka, a wealthy Brahmin who opposed educating women and Shudras.

During their meeting at Salavatika, Buddha used a powerful analogy: He asked Lohikka to imagine someone hoarding all the water of the kingdom, giving nothing to others. Eventually, without flowing, the stagnant water goes bad & becomes unusable . Through this comparison, Buddha demonstrated that restricting knowledge creates harm and stems from enmity rather than compassion.

"Just as withholding resources brings suffering," Buddha concluded, "denying knowledge to any group shows lack of concern for others' welfare and leads to an unsound doctrine built on enmity."

At Kausambi's "Beautiful Voice" vihara, Buddha encountered a priest who carried a lighted torch everywhere, believing himself unmatched in scriptural knowledge. When asked why, he said, "The world is so dark and all men are so deluded & wrapped in ignorance, so I carry this torch to illumine them." The Blessed Lord then asked if he knew the four treatises (Vidyas) in the Sacred Books—Literature (Sabdavidya), Heavenly Bodies and their Paths, Government, and Military Art. When the priest had to confess his ignorance of these subjects, he flung away his torch. The Buddha then said, "If any man, learned or not, considers himself so great as to despise others, he is like a blind man holding a candle—blind himself, he attempts to illumine others."

“In my view, a truly wise person has four different qualities. First, they help others live better lives and guide them toward good behavior. Second, they can control their thoughts well. Third, they can easily achieve deep meditation and find inner peace. Fourth, they have freed themselves from life's struggles through true understanding. These four qualities define true wisdom."

The priest agreed, acknowledging that Buddha embodied these qualities through his service to others, mental mastery, meditation skills, and complete liberation & became his follower. This dialogue highlighted how Buddha's concept of Pradnya (wisdom & understanding) differed from the Brahminical concept of Vidya (Knowledge & education)

To Cultivate Universal loving-kindness (Maitri)

Wisdom (Pradnya) is necessary, but moral conduct (Sila) is even more essential. Wisdom without moral conduct is dangerous—like a sword that can either protect or harm depending on who wields it. In the hands of someone with strong moral conduct, wisdom can save others. Without moral conduct, that same wisdom might cause harm.

This is why moral conduct surpasses wisdom in importance. While wisdom represents right thinking (Vichar Dhamma), moral conduct embodies right action (Achar Dhamma). Knowledge's value depends entirely on one's moral character. Without moral conduct, knowledge serves no purpose.

The Buddha declared, "Moral conduct is unequaled in this world. It is the beginning and the refuge, the mother of all good. It stands foremost among all virtuous qualities. Therefore, purify your moral conduct."

Scholars have debated whether wisdom (Pradnya) or compassion (Karuna) forms Buddhism's foundation. While some schools favor one over the other, both are essential pillars.

A powerful example shows Buddha's emphasis on compassion: When he found a sick patient oozing with pus whom others avoided, Buddha personally cared for him despite the man's terrible condition. While his followers recoiled, Buddha personally washed and treated the ailing man back to health. This act drew widespread attention, with many asking why such an exalted being would perform such humble service. Buddha's response revealed his view on compassion: "The purpose of Tathagata in coming into the world is to befriend those poor and helpless and unprotected, to nourish those in bodily affliction, whether they be Samanas or men of any other religion—to help the impoverished, the orphan and the aged, and to persuade others so to do."

The Buddha went beyond teaching Karuna (compassion for humans) to teach Maitri—love for all living beings. He wanted people to transcend compassion for humankind alone and cultivate loving-kindness for all creatures. "Like the earth, air, and Ganges that cannot be harmed, painted, or burned,"

Buddha said, "maintain Maitri (loving-kindness) even toward those who wrong you. Keep your mind firm as earth, pure as air, and deep as the Ganges. Let your Maitri flow endlessly, undisturbed by unpleasant acts. Those who harm others will eventually cease. Let your loving-kindness be limitless, your thoughts vast and free from hatred." "

My Dhamma teaches that Karuna (compassion) alone is insufficient—one must practice Maitri."

The Buddha shared this story to illustrate his point: "In Shravasti lived Lady Videshika, known for her gentleness. Her hardworking maid decided to test if this gentleness was genuine by coming to work progressively later each day. After two days of growing irritation, on the third day, Videshika struck her with a pin, drawing blood. The maid showed her wound to everyone, crying, 'See what the supposedly gentle one has done!' Thus, Videshika's reputation for gentleness was destroyed.

"Similarly, a monk's true nature shows only when tested. I value not those who show kindness merely for rewards, but those whose loving-kindness flows naturally from within."

"No means of acquiring religious merit equals even a sixteenth of loving-kindness. Loving-kindness, which frees the heart, surpasses all—it glows and shines forth. Like moonlight outshining all stars, and like the sun clearing the rainy season's sky, loving-kindness surpasses all other paths to merit. It illuminates completely, freeing the heart and blazing forth with unmatched radiance."

To Promote Social Equality

The Brahmin priests believed their sacred texts, the Vedas, defined the only acceptable society—one divided into four rigid classes called Chaturvarna. This system had three main rules: 1. Society must have four classes: Brahmins, Kshatriyas, Vaishyas, and Shudras. 2. Classes existed in strict hierarchy, with Brahmins at the top and Shudras at the bottom, each with different rights. 3. Each class had fixed duties: Brahmins performed religious rites and taught, Kshatriyas fought wars, Vaishyas conducted business, and Shudras were slaves & served the others. Birth determined each class & Moving between classes was forbidden. The Brahmins promoted this hierarchical system of inequality as their official doctrine.

Buddha firmly rejected the caste system and advocated for equality, challenging every argument for social division. When Assalayana confronted Buddha about caste, claiming Brahmins were superior and pure as Brahma's legitimate heirs, Buddha had a simple response. "Since Brahmin women give birth to children just like all others, how can Brahmins claim divine origin?"

"Can only Brahmins develop loving-kindness, or can all classes do this?" Buddha questioned. "All classes can," Assalayana conceded.

"Have you heard," Buddha continued, "of countries where only masters and slaves exist, and they can exchange positions?"

"Yes," replied Assalayana.

"If your caste system is perfect, why isn't it universal?" Assalayana had no answer and became Buddha's disciple.

When a Brahmin named Vasettha converted to Buddhism, others criticized him for abandoning his "superior" caste for "lower" monks. Buddha explained that Brahmins are born like everyone else, making their claims of divine birth meaningless.

Later, Another priest Esukari challenged Buddha about caste divisions, insisting Brahmins shouldn't serve others. Buddha replied, "Judge service by its results—keep what improves you, reject what harms you. This applies to everyone. Birth only gives you a name. Character determines worth, not ancestry. High ideals matter more than noble birth. No caste, no inequality, no superiority, no inferiority—all are equal. This is my position. Identify yourself with others. As they are, so am I; as I am, so are they."

Who is an outcast?

The Brahmins taught that social class (Chaturvarna) was determined by birth—Brahmins came from Brahmin parents, Kshatriyas from Kshatriya parents, and so on. They believed a person's worth derived solely from their birth status. Buddha firmly rejected this view. He taught that a person's true worth came from their actions and character, not their birth. One day while seeking alms in Shravasti, Buddha approached a Brahmin named Aggika's house. When the Brahmin angrily called Buddha an outcast, Buddha calmly asked, "Do you know what makes someone an outcast?" The Brahmin admitted he did not know, so Buddha offered to explain.

The Blessed One spoke thus: "The person who is irritable, spiteful, vicious, slanderous, perverted in views, and deceitful —know that they are an outcast. "Whoever in this world harms living beings, whether born once or twice, and shows no compassion for living creatures—know that they are an outcast.

"Whoever destroys and besieges villages and hamlets, and is known as an oppressor—know that they are an outcast.

"Whether in village or forest, whoever steals what belongs to others or takes what is not given—know that they are an outcast.

"Whoever, having taken on a debt, flees when pressed, saying 'I owe you nothing'—know that they are an outcast.

"Whoever, for mere trinkets, kills a solitary traveler on the road and robs them—know that they are an outcast.

"Whoever tells lies, whether for their own sake, for others, or for wealth—know that they are an outcast.

"Whoever, by force or consent, commits adultery with the wives of relatives or friends—know that they are an outcast.

"Whoever, though wealthy, neglects their aged parents who have passed their youth—know that they are an outcast.

"Whoever, when asked about what is right, counsels wrong and teaches deceptively—know that they are an outcast.

"No one is an outcast by birth—and no one is a Brahmin by birth." Aggika, hearing this, felt deeply ashamed of the abuse he had hurled at the Blessed One and became his follower.

Chapter 17

Was Dhamma propounded as a religion by Buddha?

While English speakers rarely think of religion as "a way to deal with suffering," this is precisely how many Indian spiritual traditions—which we now call religions—view themselves. They often liken their purpose to crossing an ocean: guiding people from suffering to peace and freedom. The concept of religion has evolved alongside human societies throughout history. In ancient times, people used religion to explain mysterious natural phenomena like storms and floods. They developed rituals and practices to try to control these events. As religion became more structured, people began believing in higher powers that governed nature. These powers were seen as both benevolent and malevolent, leading to ceremonies, prayers, and offerings to maintain their favor. Later, this evolved into the concept of a single God as creator of everything. This shift introduced new ideas, such as humans possessing souls that would be accountable to God for their earthly actions. Modern religion encompasses all these historical developments: belief in God, the soul, worship, ceremonies, and spiritual practices meant to connect with the divine.

Contemporary dictionaries offer a narrower definition—religion as belief in and worship of a supreme deity who controls human destiny. This belief-centered view emerged during Europe's Protestant Reformation and Enlightenment. As Protestant Christians emphasized faith over action and Enlightenment thinkers scrutinized religious beliefs, attention shifted from religious practices to beliefs. Though Christianity has always encompassed both belief and practice, many today reduce religions to mere belief systems—a limited view that hinders our understanding of the world's diverse faiths.

Is Buddhism a religion? The answer depends on one's definition. Buddhism differs from many faiths by not requiring belief in a controlling deity. While it includes religious practices and ceremonies, these serve as practical tools for achieving peace and ending suffering and not the ends themselves.

Buddhism is fundamentally a practical way of life. It teaches people how to live better, meditate, and understand themselves to reduce their suffering. Everything in Buddhism focuses on this goal. The Buddha taught that we shouldn't get caught up in big questions about life and the universe. Instead, we should focus on what helps us right now. To illustrate this point, Buddha told a powerful story: "Imagine someone shot with a poisoned arrow. Their friends bring a doctor to help, but the injured person says, 'Wait! Before you remove this arrow, I need to know everything about who shot me—their family background, height, hometown...' This person would die before getting all these answers." The message is clear: We must focus on solving our immediate problems rather than pondering unanswerable questions. Why didn't

Buddha answer big questions about the universe? The reason was practical—these questions didn't help people solve their actual problems.

Instead, Buddha focused on teaching four essential things: what causes suffering, why we suffer, how to stop suffering, and the steps to end suffering. Some thought Buddha didn't answer these questions because he didn't know the answers. Others believed he knew but remained silent because the answers wouldn't help anyone. But there's a deeper explanation. These questions couldn't be answered because they didn't make sense within Buddhist teaching. It's like asking what color jealousy is—the question itself is flawed because it's based on misconceptions about reality.

When people persisted with these big questions, Buddha explained their irrelevance: "Whether you believe the world goes on forever or not, you still must deal with birth, aging, death, and sorrow. I'm teaching you how to handle these real problems right now."

In Buddhism, fixating on these unanswerable metaphysical questions is part of the problem. When we get trapped in questions we can't answer, we demonstrate the very attachment to ideas that causes suffering.

Dhamma in society

Buddhism's main teaching, Dhamma, is different from regular religions. Instead of focusing on personal beliefs and worship, Dhamma teaches us how to live well with others in everyday life. Here's a simple way to understand this: If someone lived alone on an island, they would only need regular religion to connect with their God. But when people live together, they need Dhamma because it helps them get along better.

Morality & Religion

What is the place of morality in religion? Morality has no inherent place in religion. Religion's core consists of God, soul, prayers, worship, rituals, ceremonies, and sacrifices. Morality emerges only through human interaction. Religion incorporates morality merely as a secondary element to maintain peace and order. **Religion forms a triangular relationship:** "*Be good to your neighbor because you are both children of God.*" This forms religion's fundamental argument. While every religion advocates morality, it isn't religion's foundation—God is. Morality functions like a detachable wagon, connected or disconnected as circumstances require. Consequently, morality's role in religious function remains both casual and occasional, limiting its effectiveness.

What is the place of morality in Dhamma? ***Universal Morality is Dhamma, and Dhamma is Universal morality—they are one and the same.***

In Dhamma, morality occupies the central position that God holds in other religions, though Dhamma itself has no deity. Unlike traditional religions, Dhamma has no place for prayers, pilgrimages, rituals, ceremonies, or sacrifices. Morality forms the sole essence of Dhamma—without it, there would be no Dhamma. This morality stems from humanity's fundamental need to love one another. It requires no divine sanction; people should be moral not to please a god, but because mutual care and love benefit everyone.

Why does Dhamma consider universal morality as the only sacred rule?

Throughout history, societies have distinguished between sacred things (special and inviolable) and ordinary ones. When something becomes sacred, it gains protection from violation, becoming an unbreakable rule. Let's examine how morality—our sense of right and wrong—became sacred in society.

The journey began with a fundamental challenge: in nature, the strong dominate the weak. Yet early societies recognized that might shouldn't determine right. They asked, "Wouldn't protecting the vulnerable benefit everyone?" This insight led to a practical solution: establish moral rules that bind even the strongest. These rules needed sacred status—universal respect—to prevent powerful individuals from ignoring them.

However, this solution created another challenge. Different social groups developed their own moral codes. Merchants, social classes, and various groups followed different standards, leading to confusion and conflict. Why does this fragmentation matter?

When different groups follow different rules: Society cannot function cohesively, Some groups gain disproportionate power, Individual growth and development become uneven, Freedom and equality remain limited within certain groups.

The solution lies in universal morality—one set of rules that everyone follows. This approach treats humanity as a single family, governed by common principles.

This embodies Buddha's teaching: true morality (Dhamma) must be both universal and sacred, applying equally to all members of society.

Chapter 18
The Dhammapada

These verses of the Dhammapada are taken from the English translation of Khuddaka Nikaya, a collection of smaller texts within the Pali Canon of Theravada Buddhism. They provide short, impactful quotes on dealing with various human sufferings & afflictions.

On Good, Evil and Sin

1. Do good. Be no party to evil. Commit no sin. This is the Buddhist way of life.

2. When one does good, let them do it again and again, directing their heart toward it. True joy comes from accumulating good deeds.

3. Never dismiss good deeds, thinking "They won't benefit me." Just as a water pot fills drop by drop, so too does goodness grow gradually.

4. A deed well done brings no regrets—its fruits are received with delight and satisfaction.

5. When your actions bring no regrets, their rewards bring joy and contentment.

6. If you do good, do it again. Take delight in it, for the accumulation of good brings joy.

7. Even the virtuous face difficult times while their good deeds mature, but when these deeds ripen, they reap their rewards.

8. Never think lightly of good, saying "It won't come to me." Just as water drops fill a pot, the wise person becomes full of goodness, gathering it little by little.

9. The fragrance of virtue surpasses that of sandalwood, incense, lotus, or jasmine.

10. While the scent of incense and sandalwood fades, virtue's fragrance rises to the highest heights.

11. Never dismiss evil, thinking "It won't affect me." Like a water pot filling drop by drop, evil accumulates gradually.

12. Avoid deeds that bring regret, whose fruits are received with tears and sorrow.

13. When one speaks or acts with evil intent, suffering follows as surely as a wheel follows the ox that pulls the cart.

14. Shun evil. Avoid negligence. Reject false ideas.

15. Pursue excellence and suppress evil thoughts. Those who hesitate to do good find their minds drawn to evil. 16. Avoid actions that bring regret, whose consequences lead to tears and grief.

17. Even wrongdoers experience happiness while their evil deeds remain unripe, but when these deeds mature, they must face their consequences.

18. Never think lightly of evil, saying "It won't affect me." As water drops fill a pot, so does a fool become full of evil, gathering it little by little.

19. Hasten toward good and guard your thoughts from evil. If one practices good deeds lazily, their mind drifts toward wrong.

20. If you commit a wrong, do not repeat it. Take no pleasure in wrongdoing, for evil's accumulation brings pain.

21. Follow virtue's path, not sin's. The virtuous find peace in this world.

22. From desire springs sorrow; from desire springs fear. One wholly free from desire knows neither sorrow nor fear.

23. Hunger is the worst affliction, existence the greatest burden. Understanding this truth, one realizes nirvana is the highest happiness.

24. Evil done by oneself, self-created and self-nurtured, crushes the doer as a diamond breaks even the hardest stone.

25. One whose wickedness grows great brings themselves low, just as a creeper strangles the tree it embraces. 26. Harmful and selfish acts come easily; what benefits and serves good is harder to do.

On Craving and Lust

1. Do not be possessed by craving or lust. This is the Buddhist way of life.

2. Even abundant wealth cannot satisfy desire. The wise person knows that desires bring only grief and dissatisfaction.

3. Even heavenly pleasures bring no delight to the enlightened; their joy comes from ending craving—such is the disciple of the Buddha, the Supremely Awakened One.

4. From craving springs sorrow, from craving springs fear. One who is wholly free from craving knows neither sorrow nor fear.

5. Those who chase vanity and pleasure, forgetting life's true purpose, will come to envy those devoted to meditation.

6. Avoid attachment to anything, for loss brings pain. Those free from love and hate have no bonds.

7. From pleasure comes grief, from pleasure comes fear; one free from pleasure knows neither grief nor fear.

8. From attachment comes grief, from attachment comes fear; one free from attachment knows neither grief nor fear.

9. From lust comes grief, from lust comes fear; one free from lust knows neither grief nor fear. 10. From greed comes grief, from greed comes fear; one free from greed knows neither grief nor fear.

11. The world cherishes those who possess virtue and intelligence, who are just, speak truth, and mind their own affairs.

12. As loved ones welcome home one who returns safely from afar, so too do good deeds welcome those who have done good and departed this world.

On Hurt and Ill-will

1. Cause no hurt; cherish no ill-will. This is the Buddhist Way of Life.

2. Is there anyone in this world so blameless that they give no cause for reproach, as a spirited horse gives no reason for the lash?

3. Through confidence, virtue, energy, meditation, investigation of Truth, perfection in knowledge and conduct, and mindfulness—leave this great suffering behind.

4. The most excellent of ascetic practices is forbearance and long-suffering; "Nibbana is most excellent of all," so says the Buddha. One who hurts others is no ascetic; one who causes another's suffering is no disciple.

5. To speak no ill, to do no harm, to practice restraint according to the discipline—this is the Buddha's counsel.

6. Neither kill nor cause slaughter.

7. One who seeks happiness by neither punishing nor killing beings who also long for happiness will find happiness.

8. If, like a broken metal plate, you utter nothing, then you have reached Nibbana; anger is unknown to you.

9. One who inflicts pain on innocent and harmless persons will soon face grief.

10. One who, clothed in the fine garment of tranquility, is quiet, subdued, restrained, chaste, and has ceased finding fault with all other beings—they indeed are an ascetic (Samana), a friar (Bhikku).

11. Is there in this world any person so restrained by shame that they do not invite reproof, as a noble horse the whip?

12. If someone wrongs a harmless, pure, and innocent person, the evil returns to that fool, like fine dust thrown against the wind.

On Anger and Enmity

1. Cherish no anger. Forget your enmities. Win your enemies with love. This is the Buddhist Way of Life.

2. The fire of anger must be stilled.

3. For one who dwells on thoughts like "They reviled me, maltreated me, overpowered me, robbed me," anger will never be stilled.

4. But for one who does not harbor such thoughts, anger subsides.

5. When enemies work evil against each other, when haters confront haters, who truly bears the evil?

6. Let one overcome anger with love, evil with good, greed with generosity, and lies with truth.

7. Speak truthfully, resist anger, and give freely when asked for little.

8. Let one abandon anger, forsake pride, and break free from all bondage. Those who claim nothing as their own, who are not attached to name and form, suffer no affliction.

9. One who restrains rising anger—like a skilled charioteer controlling a racing chariot—is a true master. Others merely hold the reins.

10. Conquest breeds enmity; the defeated lie in misery. But the peaceful one rests happily, having set aside both victory and defeat.

11. No fire burns like lust, no misfortune equals hatred. There is no suffering like existence itself, no happiness higher than Nibbana's peace.

12. For hatred never ceases through hatred—this is an ancient truth. Only through love does hatred cease.

On Mind and Impurities

1. We are what our minds make us.

2. Training the mind to seek good is the first step on the path of Righteousness.

3. This is the central teaching of the Buddhist Way of Life.

4. In all things, mind is the primal element. Mind is supreme.

5. When one speaks or acts with evil intent, suffering follows as closely as the wheel follows the hoof of the ox that draws the cart.

6. When one speaks or acts with an upright mind, happiness follows as faithfully as one's never-departing shadow.

7. This restless, unsteady mind is difficult to guard and guide —yet the wise person makes it straight, as a fletcher straightens an arrow.

8. As a fish thrashes when cast upon dry land, so does the mind flounder when pulled from its desires.

9. Hard to control and unstable is this mind, forever seeking pleasure. Yet it is good to tame it, for a disciplined mind brings happiness.

10. Make yourself an island, strive diligently; when your impurities are purged and you are free from guilt, you shall enter the heavenly realm of the elect.

11. Let the wise person remove impurities from themselves gradually, as a smith removes impurities from silver—one by one, little by little, moment by moment.

12. As rust arising from iron eventually destroys it, so do one's own misdeeds lead to the path of destruction.

13. Yet there is one taint worse than all others: ignorance is the greatest taint. O seekers! Cast off this taint and become pure.

14. Life comes easily to one without shame—a scavenger, a troublemaker, insolent and debased.

15. But life is challenging for the modest person who seeks purity, who remains detached, peaceful, unblemished, and wise.

16. One who takes life, speaks falsely, takes what is not given, or violates another's marriage;

17. And one who indulges in intoxicating drinks—such a person digs their own grave in this very world.

18. Know this: those without self-control live in misery. Take care that greed and vice do not bring lasting sorrow.

19. The world gives according to its faith or pleasure; one who envies others' food and drink finds no peace, day or night.

20. One who has uprooted such envy finds true rest, both day and night.

21. No fire burns like passion; no flood surges like greed.

22. We easily see others' faults while overlooking our own. We sift through others' flaws like chaff, yet hide our own as a cheat conceals loaded dice.

23. One who dwells on others' faults and takes offense easily feeds their own passions, moving further from liberation.

24. Abstain from evil, nurture goodness, purify your thoughts—this is the Buddha's teaching.

On Self and Self-Conquest

1. If one has a self, one must practice self-conquest. This is the Buddhist Way of Life.

2. Self is the lord of self—who else could be the lord? With self well-subdued, one finds a master such as few can find.

3. The foolish one who scorns the rule of the venerable (arahat), of the elect (ariya), of the virtuous, and follows false doctrine, bears fruit to their own destruction, like the fruits of the Katthaka reed.

4. By oneself evil is done, by oneself one suffers; by oneself evil is left undone, by oneself one is purified. The pure and impure stand and fall by themselves—no one can purify another.

5. One who seeks uncontrolled pleasures, is immoderate in food, idle and weak, will surely be overthrown by their own excess, as wind throws down a weak tree.

6. One who lives without seeking pleasures, with senses well controlled, moderate in food, faithful and strong, will not be overthrown, just as wind cannot throw down a rocky mountain.

7. If you hold yourself dear, keep close watch upon yourself.

8. First establish yourself in what is right, then counsel others. Let not the wise person give cause for reproach.

9. The self, they say, is hard to control. If one shapes oneself as one counsels others, then well-controlled, one will have mastery over others.

10. Though one may conquer thousands upon thousands in battle, the greatest warrior is one who conquers oneself.

11. Truly, oneself is the guardian of oneself. What other guardian could there be? With oneself well-guarded, one gains a protector unlike any other.

On Wisdom, Justice and Good Company

1. Be wise, be just, and choose good company. This is the Buddhist Way of Life.

2. If you see an intelligent person who points out what to avoid and offers correction, follow them as you would one who

reveals hidden treasures—you will benefit, not suffer, from their guidance.

3. Let them advise, teach, and discourage improper actions—the good will love them, while the bad will hate them.

4. Do not befriend evil-doers or those of low character; befriend the virtuous and seek the company of the best.

5. One who absorbs the Dhamma lives happily with a serene mind; the sage always rejoices in the Dhamma as taught by the enlightened.

6. Well-makers guide water, fletchers bend arrows, carpenters shape wood—wise people shape themselves.

7. Like a solid rock unshaken by wind, the wise remain steady amid blame and praise.

8. After hearing the Dhamma, wise people become serene, like a deep, smooth, and still lake.

9. Good people walk mindfully in all circumstances. They speak not from desire for pleasure, and whether touched by happiness or sorrow, remain neither elated nor depressed.

10. "It is sweet as honey," thinks the fool while evil has not yet ripened. But when it ripens, the fool comes to grief.

11. A fool knows not when they commit evil deeds, but the wicked burn by their own actions, as if consumed by fire.

12. Long is the night to one who is awake; long is a mile to one who is tired; long is life to the foolish who do not know the true Dhamma.

13. If a traveler meets neither better nor equal companions, let them journey alone—there is no companionship with fools.

14. "These sons belong to me, and this wealth belongs to me"—with such thoughts a fool is tormented. They do not even own themselves; how much less their sons and wealth?

15. The fool who knows their foolishness is wise at least to that extent. But a fool who thinks themselves wise is truly called a fool.

16. A fool may associate with a wise person their whole life yet perceive truth as little as a spoon tastes soup.

17. An intelligent person, spending just a moment with the wise, quickly perceives truth as the tongue tastes soup.

18. Fools of poor understanding are their own worst enemies, for they do evil deeds that bear bitter fruits.

19. That deed is not well done which brings remorse, whose reward one receives with tears and grief.

20. Know that a deed is well done when one does not repent, and its reward brings gladness and joy.

21. When an evil deed becomes known and turns to sorrow for the fool, it destroys their good fortune and splits their head.

22. Let the fool wish for false reputation, precedence among others, authority in monasteries, and worship from all.

23. A person is not an elder merely because their head is grey; though their age may be ripe, they are called "old-and-vain."

24. One who embodies truth, virtue, compassion, restraint,

and moderation—who is free from impurity and wise—is called an elder.

25. An envious, stingy, dishonest person does not become respectable through mere talk or appearance.

26. One in whom these faults are destroyed at the root, who is free from hatred and wise—such a one is called respectable.

27. A person is not just if they enforce matters through violence. The just one distinguishes right from wrong, learns and guides others through Dhamma rather than force, guards the Dhamma, and acts with intelligence.

28. One is not learned merely through much talking. The learned one is patient, free from hatred and fear.

29. One is not a supporter of the Dhamma through much talking. Even with little learning, one who embodies the Dhamma and never neglects it is its true supporter.

30. If one finds a prudent companion who walks wisely and lives soberly, walk with them—overcoming all dangers, happy yet mindful.

31. If one finds no prudent companion, walk alone—like a king who has left his conquered country, like an elephant in the forest.

32. Better to live alone than to keep company with fools. Walk alone, commit no sin, with few wishes—like an elephant in the forest.

33. Friends are welcome when the occasion arises; enjoyment is pleasant, whatever its cause. A good deed is pleasant, especially at death's hour. Pleasant too is the end of all grief.

34. Pleasant in this world is the state of a mother, pleasant the state of a father, pleasant the state of a Samana.

35. Pleasant is virtue lasting to old age, pleasant is firmly rooted faith, pleasant is the attainment of intelligence, pleasant is avoiding sins.

36. Walking with fools brings suffering; their company, like that of an enemy, brings pain. Company with the wise brings pleasure, like meeting with kin.

37. Therefore, follow the wise, intelligent, learned, enduring, and dutiful. Follow such good and wise ones as the moon follows the path of stars.

38. Follow not after vanity, nor the pleasures of love and lust. The earnest one obtains abundant joy.

39. When the learned person drives away vanity through earnestness, they climb wisdom's heights. Free from sorrow, they look upon the sorrowing crowd as one on a mountain looks upon those on the plain.

40. Earnest among the thoughtless, awake among the sleepers, the wise advance swiftly, leaving others behind.

On Mindfulness

1. In everything be thoughtful; in everything be mindful; in all things be earnest and bold. This is the Buddhist Way of Life.

2. All that we are arises from our thoughts—our very being is founded upon and shaped by them. When one speaks or acts with an evil thought, pain follows. When one speaks or acts

with a pure thought, happiness follows. Therefore, pure thoughts are essential.

3. Be not thoughtless—watch your thoughts! Free yourself from harmful ways, as an elephant pulls itself from mud.

4. Let the wise guard their thoughts, which are subtle, elusive, and swift in their movement. Well-guarded thoughts bring happiness.

5. As rain penetrates an ill-thatched house, passion penetrates an unreflecting mind.

6. As rain cannot breach a well-thatched house, passion cannot breach a well-reflecting mind.

7. Once my mind wandered freely, following its every whim and desire; but now I shall master it completely, as a mahout with a hook controls a wild elephant.

8. It is good to tame the mind, though it is difficult to hold and control in its rushing. A tamed mind brings happiness.

9. Those who restrain their far-wandering mind will break free from temptation's bonds.

10. When faith wavers, when one lacks knowledge of true Dhamma, when peace of mind is disturbed—wisdom cannot fully bloom.

11. Whatever harm a hater may inflict upon another hater, or an enemy upon an enemy, a misguided mind inflicts even greater harm upon oneself.

12. Neither mother, father, nor any other relative can bestow as much benefit as a well-directed mind.

On Vigilance & Courage

1. When vigilant, the wise rise above negligence. From their tower of wisdom, they look down—free from sorrow—upon humanity's suffering. Like one atop a mountain, they observe the foolish in the valley below.

2. Vigilant among the negligent, awake among the sleeping—like a swift horse outpacing a worn-out nag—so move the wise.

3. Guard against negligence. Shun the lures of sensual pleasure. The vigilant dedicate themselves to meditation.

4. Earnestness leads to immortality; heedlessness to death. Those who persist in earnestness do not die, while the heedless are as if already dead.

5. Do not abandon your purpose for another's, however great that other purpose may be. Once you find your goal, hold to it firmly.

6. Stay watchful! Cast off indolence! Walk the True Path! Those who follow it live happily in this world.

7. Idleness brings disgrace; persistent sloth breeds corruption. Through determined effort and insight, remove the poisoned arrow of indolence.

8. Shun negligence. Resist the pleasures of the flesh. The vigilant who devote themselves to meditation achieve boundless happiness.

9. When earnest people rouse themselves—remaining mindful, acting purely and thoughtfully, practicing self-restraint, and living according to Dhamma—their glory grows.

On Sorrow and Happiness

1. Poverty gives rise to sorrow.

2. Yet the mere absence of poverty does not guarantee happiness.

3. Happiness stems not from a high standard of living, but from a high standard of culture.

4. This is the Buddhist Way of Life.

5. Hunger is the worst affliction.

6. Health is the greatest gift, contentment the greatest wealth, trust the finest relationship, and Nibbana the highest happiness.

7. We must learn to live happily, free from hatred toward those who hate us.

8. We must learn to live happily, maintaining wellness among the sick.

9. We must learn to live happily, staying free from greed among the greedy.

10. Passion ruins mankind as weeds destroy fields; thus, charity given to the passionless brings great reward.

11. Vanity damages mankind as weeds ravage fields; thus, charity given to the humble brings great reward.

12. Lust ruins mankind as weeds destroy fields; thus, charity given to the pure brings great reward.

13. Charity to Dhamma surpasses all gifts. The sweetness of

Dhamma surpasses all sweetness. The delight in Dhamma surpasses all delights.

14. Victory breeds hatred, for the defeated dwell in misery. One who transcends both victory and defeat finds happiness in contentment.

15. No fire burns like passion, no affliction cuts like hatred, no burden weighs like this body, no peace surpasses inner tranquility.

16. Dwell not on others' faults or their actions and inactions. Look instead to what you yourself have done or left undone.

17. Life presents challenges for the modest—those who seek purity, detachment, solitude, cleanliness, and wisdom.

18. Who among us is so blameless they deserve no reproach? Be like a spirited horse that needs no lash—fiery yet disciplined.

19. Speak harshly to none, for harsh words return as harsh words. Angry speech brings pain, and violence begets violence.

20. Liberty, courtesy, goodwill, and selflessness—these are to the world what the linchpin is to the chariot.

21. This is the Buddhist Way of Life.

On Hypocrisy

1. Let no one speak falsely, lead others to falsehood, or approve of those who deceive. All forms of lying and deception must be cast aside.

2. The Perfect One's words and actions are in harmony—as he speaks, so he acts; as he acts, so he speaks. This unity of word and deed is why he is called the Perfect One. This is the Buddhist Way of Life.

On following the Right Way

1. Choose the Right Way and depart not from it.

2. There are many paths, but not all lead to the Right Way.

3. The Right Path brings happiness not just to the few, but to all.

4. It must be good at the beginning, good in the middle, and good at the end.

5. To follow the Right Way is to lead the Buddhist Way of Life.

6. The best way is the Eightfold Way; the best of truths, the Four Words; the best of virtues, passionlessness; the best of men, he who has eyes to see.

7. This is the way—there is no other—that leads to the purifying of intelligence. Go on this path.

8. If you go on this way, you will make an end of pain. The way was preached by me when I had understood the removal of the thorns.

9. You yourself must make an effort. The Tathagatas are only preachers.

10. "All created things perish"—he who knows and sees this becomes passive in pain.

11. "All forms are unreal"—he who knows and sees this becomes passive in pain.

12. He who does not rouse himself when it is time to rise, who, though young and strong, is full of sloth, whose will and thought are weak—that lazy and idle man never finds the way to knowledge.

13. Watching his speech, well restrained in mind, let a man never commit any wrong with his body. Let a man but keep these three roads of action clear, and he will achieve the way which is taught by the wise.

14. Through real knowledge is gained, through lack of real knowledge is lost. Let a man who knows this double path of gain and loss thus place himself that knowledge may grow.

15. Cut out the love of self like an autumn lotus with thy hand! Cherish the road of peace. Nirvana has been shown by the Sugata.

16. Do not follow the evil law! Do not live on in thoughtlessness! Do not follow false doctrine!

17. Rouse thyself! Do not be idle! Follow the law of virtue! The virtuous rest in bliss in this world.

18. He who formerly was reckless and afterwards became sober brightens up this world, like the moon when freed from clouds.

19. He whose evil deeds are covered by good deeds brightens up this world, like the moon when freed from clouds.

20. If a man has transgressed the one law and speaks lies, there is no evil he will not do.

21. Those who are ever watchful, who study day and night, and who strive after Nirvana—their passions will come to an end.

22. This is an old saying: "They blame him who sits silent, they blame him who speaks much, they also blame him who says little." There is no one on earth who is not blamed.

23. There never was, there never will be, nor is there now, a man who is always blamed, or a man who is always praised.

24. Beware of the anger of the tongue, and control thy tongue. Leave the sins of the mind, and practice virtue with thy mind.

25. Earnestness is the path of Nirvana, thoughtlessness the path of death. Those who are in earnest do not die; those who are thoughtless are as if dead already.

On Truth & Falsehood

1. Those who mistake falsehood for truth and truth for falsehood possess wrong-mindedness—they shall never discover truth.

2. Those who see truth as truth and falsehood as falsehood possess right-mindedness—they shall find truth.

3. Just as rain seeps into a poorly thatched house, craving penetrates an untrained mind.

4. Just as rain cannot breach a well-thatched house, craving cannot enter a well-trained mind.

5. Arise! Be vigilant! Follow the Good Way of the Teaching! One who walks this path finds happiness in this world and all worlds.

6. Walk the Good Way of the Teaching; avoid the path of evil. One who follows these teachings lives in joy, both in this world and beyond. This is the Buddhist way of life.

Chapter 19

Buddhas Sermons, continued

The Happy Householder

Once Anathapindika came to where the Buddha was, made obeisance, and took a seat at his side. Anathapindika wished to understand what constituted a householder's happiness and asked the Buddha to explain this, the Lord spoke of four kinds of happiness:

First is the happiness of possession. A householder finds joy in wealth justly and righteously acquired through great industry, amassed by strength of arm, and earned by the sweat of his brow. He gains happiness thinking, "I have earned this wealth honestly."

Second is the happiness of enjoyment. A householder who has justly earned his wealth finds joy in using it wisely and performing acts of merit. He gains happiness thinking, "I am using my honest wealth to do good."

Third is the happiness of freedom from debt. A householder finds joy in owing nothing to anyone, great or small. He gains happiness thinking, "I am free of all debts."

Fourth is the happiness of blamelessness. A householder finds joy in living with blameless actions of body, blameless speech, and blameless thoughts. "Truly, Anathapindika," said the Lord, "these four kinds of happiness are available to any householder who strives for them."

Husband and Wife

Once while traveling between Madhura and Neranja, the Buddha rested under a tree. Several householders and their wives approached him to ask about marriage. The Buddha responded: "Householders, marriages take four forms: a vile man with a vile woman, a vile man with a goddess, a god with a vile woman, and a god with a goddess."

"A vile marriage occurs when both spouses engage in killing, stealing, lying, and evil deeds—living with avarice and abusing others."

"When a wicked husband has a virtuous wife who abstains from evil and lives righteously, we see a vile man with a goddess."

"When a righteous husband who avoids all evil has a wicked wife who engages in killing, stealing, and lives with avarice, we find a god with a vile woman."

"When both spouses are virtuous, avoiding evil deeds and living righteously—without avarice or abuse—this creates a union of a god with a goddess." "These, householders, are the four ways of living together."

Twelve Causes of Man's Downfall

One night at Anathapindika's monastery in Shravasti, a radiant Deva approached the Blessed One. The Deva bowed and asked, "O Gotama, what causes a person's downfall?"

The Blessed One replied: "Easily known is the progressive one, easily known is the declining one. A lover of the Dhamma progresses, while one who hates the Dhamma declines.

"One who befriends the vicious and finds no joy in the virtuous, who favors the teachings of the wicked—this is the second cause of downfall.

"One who is lazy, seeks idle company, shows no initiative, remains slothful, and gives in to anger—this is the third cause of downfall.

"One who, despite having wealth, neglects to support their elderly parents—this is the fourth cause of downfall.

"One who deceives through falsehood a Brahmana, an ascetic, or any other holy seeker—this is the fifth cause of downfall.

"One who possesses great wealth, gold, and food, yet enjoys these pleasures alone—this is the sixth cause of downfall.

"One who boasts of birth, wealth, or clan while looking down upon their own kin—this is the seventh cause of downfall.

"One who wastes their life in debauchery, drink, and gambling, squandering all they own—this is the eighth cause of downfall.

"One who, unsatisfied with their own spouse, seeks pleasure with courtesans and others' wives—this is the ninth cause of downfall.

"One who places in authority a wasteful, unrestrained woman or man—this is the eleventh cause of downfall.

"One who, though of modest means, harbors grand ambitions and, being of warrior birth, craves sovereignty—this is the twelfth cause of downfall.

"Know these causes of downfall, noble Deva. Overcome them, and you shall find salvation."

The Wicked Man

The Blessed Lord, while on a journey, gave his customary discourse to the Bhikkhus who were accompanying him.

"Do you know how to recognize a wicked man?" the Lord asked the Bhikkhus. "No, Lord," they replied.

"I will tell you the characteristics of a wicked man:

1. They love pointing out other people's faults. Without anyone asking, they'll tell you what's wrong with others. If you ask them about someone, they'll gladly list every bad thing that person has done.

2. They never want to say anything good about others. Even when asked directly about someone's good qualities, they'll only say nice things reluctantly and without enthusiasm.

3. They hide their own faults. When asked about their mistakes, they try to cover them up or make them seem smaller than they are. They never admit their wrongs openly.

4. They brag about themselves constantly. They talk about how great they are without anyone asking. When someone does ask about their good qualities, they go on and on about themselves without any modesty.

The Best Man

The Blessed One, while journeying, gave his customary discourse to the accompanying Bhikkhus: "There are four types of people in this world, brethren: First, one who strives neither for their own welfare nor others'; second, one who strives for others' welfare but neglects their own; third, one who strives for their own welfare but neglects others'; and fourth, one who strives for both their own welfare and that of others.

The person who strives for neither their own welfare nor others' is like a torch from a funeral pyre—lit at both ends and smeared with dung in the middle. Such a person kindles no light in village or forest, serving neither themselves nor the world. The one who strives for others' welfare at the expense of their own shows noble excellence. Yet brethren, of all four types, the person who strives for both their own welfare and that of others stands supreme—this is the highest and noblest path."

Need for Making Good Resolutions and Doing Good Deeds

Once when he was at Shravasti in Jeta's Grove, the Buddha said to the Brethren: "Do not fear doing good deeds, my friends. When I speak of good deeds, I speak of happiness—

the things that bring joy and contentment. From my own experience, I can tell you that doing good has brought me happiness for many years.

"When I ask myself, 'Why am I so happy and content?' The answer is always clear: it comes from three simple practices—being generous to others, maintaining self-discipline, and exercising self-control.

"Every morning becomes beautiful when we help others. When we give to those who deserve it, perform good deeds, speak kind words, think positive thoughts, and maintain good intentions—all these bring happiness to those who practice them.

"Those who live this way find true happiness and success. May you too find success, good health, and happiness with your loved ones."

"Brethren, there is a great need for good resolutions to be made and observed for a pure and happy life.

"I will tell you what your resolutions should be. Resolve that: 'Throughout my life, may I support my parents. May I respect the head of my clan. May I speak gently. May I speak no evil of others. Clearing my heart of selfishness, may I dwell at home generous and pure-handed, delighting in giving up, may I be worthy of others' trust, finding joy in sharing gifts with others. Throughout my life, may I be free from anger, and if anger arises, may I quickly subdue it.'

"These are the seven resolutions, Brethren, by undertaking and following which you will attain the state of happiness and purity."

What is Righteousness

Once when the Lord was on an alms-pilgrimage in Sala village of Kosala, The priests asked the Blessed One to explain the meaning of righteousness.

The Buddha said: "There are three forms of unrighteousness and wickedness of the body, four of speech, and three of thoughts.

"*Concerning bodily unrighteousness,* a person may (i) take life —acting as a hunter with blood-stained hands, killing and slaying without mercy toward living creatures; or (ii) steal—taking what is not given, whether in village or jungle; or (iii) commit sexual misconduct—having relations with those under family protection or those who are betrothed and wear betrothal garlands.

"*Regarding unrighteousness of speech,* a man may: (i) be a liar—giving false testimony before assemblies, meetings, or councils by claiming knowledge he lacks, denying knowledge he has, claiming to have seen what he hasn't, or denying what he has seen, all for personal gain or others' benefit; (ii) be a slanderer—spreading words that create discord between people, destroying harmony and stirring up strife, finding joy in division; (iii) speak with a bitter tongue—using harsh, hurtful words that wound others and provoke anger; or (iv) be an idle chatterer—speaking without purpose, discussing trivial matters instead of the Doctrine or Rule, and engaging in untimely, frivolous, and unprofitable talk.

"*Regarding unrighteousness of thought,* a man may: (i) be covetous—constantly desiring others' possessions as his own; (ii) be malevolent in heart—harboring ill will toward other beings and wishing for their destruction; or (iii) hold wrong views—believing that good and evil deeds have no consequences, denying the existence of this world and others, refusing to acknowledge parents or relations in other realms, and rejecting the existence of genuine spiritual seekers who have discovered these truths through their own efforts and shared them with others."

"Conversely, there are three forms of righteousness and goodness for the body, four for speech, and three for thoughts.

"*Regarding bodily righteousness,* a person (i) refrains from killing—setting aside all weapons to live with innocence and mercy, showing kindness and compassion toward all living beings; (ii) abstains from theft, accepting only what others freely give, living honestly; and (iii) avoids sexual misconduct by respecting those under family protection and those who are betrothed.

"*Regarding righteousness in speech,* (i) a man abstains from lying—when giving testimony before any assembly, meeting, council, or guild, he speaks truthfully, acknowledging what he knows and doesn't know, what he has and hasn't seen, never lying for personal gain or others' benefit. (ii) He avoids slander, refusing to spread words that create discord; instead, he promotes harmony and mends friendships, finding joy in unity. (iii) His speech is gentle and kind—his words are pleasant, friendly, and welcoming to all. (iv) He shuns idle chatter, speaking only what is timely, truthful, and meaningful, discussing the Doctrine and Rule with words that enlighten and benefit others.

"*Regarding righteousness in thoughts,* (i) a man remains free from covetousness, never craving others' possessions. (ii) He harbors no ill will; instead, he wishes for all beings to live in peace and happiness, free from hostility and harm. (iii) He upholds right views and clear understanding. "This is what I mean by righteousness and unrighteousness."

Then the Buddha addressed the lay brethren of Pataligama: "Householders, consider the losses that befall the wicked and immoral person. "Through laziness, such a person suffers great loss of wealth. Their evil reputation spreads far, bringing shame before all. When they enter any company—whether nobles, Brahmins, householders, or recluses—they enter timidly, with a confused mind and lacking courage. This is the third loss. Finally, they die with a troubled mind, finding no peace. This is the fourth loss. Such, householders, are the consequences that befall one who lives wickedly."

"Now consider the rewards of one who lives virtuously. Through diligent effort, the virtuous person gains great wealth. Their good reputation spreads, bringing honor everywhere. When they enter any company—whether nobles, Brahmins, householders, or recluses—they enter boldly and confidently. At life's end, they enjoy peace of mind and depart with an untroubled spirit."

"The fool who does evil remains blind to their folly: their own deeds consume them like fire." "One who harms the harmless and innocent soon faces grievous disaster—a troubled mind, loss of loved ones, and loss of all wealth."

Do not abandon Righteousness citing family reasons

At the Bamboo Grove in Rajagraha, Sariputta learned from an almsman about Dhananjani, a corrupt Landlord who exploited others.

"How is his spiritual progress?" asked Sariputta.

"Poor—he is dishonest and has married an impious woman after his pious wife's death" replied the almsman.

Concerned, Sariputta went to seek him out in Rajagraha. He found Dhananjani watching his cows being milked outside the city gates. When Dhananjani offered him milk, Sariputta gently reminded him that Bhikkus dont eat after mid day & suggested they meet later under a tree instead. "Are you living righteously, Dhananjani?" Sariputta asked.

"How can I, with so many to support—family, servants, friends, ancestors, gods, and king?"

"Would your family duties excuse you from legal punishment?" "No." "Would anyone's pleas change this?"

"No."

"Then which is better—wrongdoing or righteousness?"

"Righteousness," admitted Dhananjani.

"You can support your family righteously, can you not?" "Yes, Sariputta." Satisfied, the Brahmin departed.

How to Reach Perfection in Righteous Conduct

At Shravasti, Dhammika and other followers sought the Lord's guidance. "Great Teacher, your wisdom surpasses all others. Please instruct us. How can we achieve perfect righteousness?" asked Dhammika.

The Lord replied: "I shall teach you the path of righteous conduct. Do not kill, harm, or incite violence against any being. Accept only what is freely given—neither steal nor condone theft. Honor marriage bonds and abstain from lust. Speak truthfully in all matters and shun falsehood. Abstain from alcohol, which clouds the mind and corrupts behavior. For through drink comes folly and wrongdoing—shun this deceptive pleasure."

"Observe these five precepts: abstain from killing, stealing, lying, drinking, and sexual misconduct.

"Live modestly: eschew luxuries, rest simply, maintain weekly observances, and celebrate festivals with devotion. Share sustenance with everyone, expressing gratitude and devotion.

"Honor your parents and work with integrity. This path leads to higher realms."

On Elephants & Friends

“Stay strong when others criticize you, just like an elephant remains calm during battle. When someone stays peaceful despite harsh words, they show true strength - like a well-trained elephant carrying its rider. Good horses are valuable & strong elephants are amazing. But someone who can control their own mind is even more impressive.”

“But animals can't teach us inner peace - only learning to control our own thoughts can do that. Keep working to become better. Watch your thoughts carefully, and break free from bad habits, just as you'd help pull an elephant from mud”.

“If you find a wise and honest friend, walk life's path together happily. But if you can't find a good friend, it's better to go alone - like a king avoiding danger or an elephant walking peacefully in the forest.”

“It's better to be alone than to spend time with foolish people. Live simply and avoid doing wrong - like a peaceful elephant in the forest. Clear your mind of harmful thoughts.”

Here's what to do:

Stay peaceful when others are harmful.

Don't kill, even if others do.

Don't steal, even if others do.

Live a good life, even if others don't.

Don't lie or gossip, even if others do.

Be happy with what you have, even if others are greedy.

Be kind, even if others are mean.

Follow the right path: think clearly, make good choices, tell the truth, act well, work honestly, try your best, and stay focused - even when others don't.

Stand up for what's right, even when others are confused or silent.

Stay active when others are lazy.

Stay humble when others are proud.

Keep your mind clear when others are uncertain.

When you see others being angry, hateful, jealous, greedy, dishonest, proud, careless, or confused - be different.

Choose to be peaceful, loving, supportive, generous, honest, humble, careful, and wise.

Why Clear Thinking is supreme

Of the Noble Eightfold Path, Right Outlook stands supreme. Right thinking forms the foundation of the higher life—it is knowledge, not ignorance, that lights the way. Without understanding, all evil takes root. To develop Right Outlook, one must recognize life's phenomena as governed by causality. This means seeing clearly the law of cause and effect.

"When someone follows perverted views—with perverted aims, speech, actions, living, effort, attention, and contemplation—their knowledge and liberation become twisted. Every deed, word, and thought born from such views leads to suffering. Every action, aspiration, and resolve brings what is distasteful, unpleasing, repulsive, unprofitable, and painful. Why? Because their view itself is corrupted."

Merely being right is insufficient. A baby may happen to be right, yet lacks true understanding. To be truly right, one must comprehend what makes it right.

"Ananda, who deserves to be called an almsman? Only one who has mastered the distinction between what is rationally possible and what is not."

It is Not What You Eat that Makes You Holy

A priest approached the Lord to discuss how food influences character, claiming that a vegetarian diet leads to virtue while eating meat is wrong. The Lord responded that true impurity lies not in what one eats, but in harmful actions: killing, stealing, lying, cruelty, anger, pride, and deceit. He explained that neither dietary restrictions nor religious rituals can purify someone lacking inner truth.

"Control your senses, seek truth, and be kind," the Lord counseled. "One who overcomes life's challenges remains pure, regardless of their diet." Moved by these teachings, the brahman priest asked to become an Almsman.

Amagandha, a vegetarian Brahmin ascetic from the Himalayas, made yearly visits to a village where locals hosted his group for four months. After the Blessed Lord's teachings converted the villagers, Amagandha's group received a notably cooler welcome. Learning that the Lord permitted meat-eating, Amagandha confronted him at Jeta Vana: "The righteous eat only simple vegetarian foods obtained honestly. You eat meat yet claim to be pure. What then is impurity?"

The Lord replied: "Taking life, beating, cutting, binding, stealing, lying, fraud, deception, false knowledge, and adultery —this is impurity, not the eating of flesh.

"Those who are unrestrained in sensual pleasures, greedy for sweet things, engaged in impure actions, hold nihilistic views, and follow crooked paths—this is impurity, not the eating of flesh.

"Those who are rude, harsh, backbiting, treacherous, unkind, excessively proud, and ungenerous—this is impurity, not the eating of flesh.

"Anger, pride, stubbornness, hostility, deceit, envy, boasting, excessive ego, and associating with the unrighteous—this is impurity, not the eating of flesh.

"Those who evade their debts, slander and deceive in their dealings, who pretend and commit vile acts—this is impurity, not the eating of flesh.

"Those who harm living beings without restraint, who steal others' possessions, who are immoral, cruel, harsh, and disrespectful—this is impurity not the eating of flesh.

"Those who attack beings out of greed or hatred, who constantly turn toward evil—they descend into darkness after death and fall into hell—this is impurity, not the eating of flesh.

"No outward practice—whether abstaining from meat, going naked, shaving one's head, wearing ashes or skins, or performing rituals—can purify those filled with doubt.

"The wise one lives with controlled senses, follows the Dhamma, embraces gentleness, and releases attachments and sorrows, not clinging to experiences. "Evil deeds, not diet, make one impure."

Purpose of practising the Holy Life

Once, while traveling, the Blessed Lord gave his customary discourse to the accompanying Bhikkhus. Addressing them, the Lord said: "O brethren, we do not practice this holy life to deceive others, seek favor, gain benefits, or achieve fame. Nor do we practice it to avoid controversy or gain recognition. Rather, brethren, we practice this holy life to master our body and speech, cleanse ourselves of corruption, and free ourselves from the bonds of craving."

Do Not Depend on the Favour of Princes

While staying at the Bamboo Grove in Rajagraha, the Buddha learned that Prince Ajatasatru was helping Devadatta, who was against the Buddha's teachings. The prince gave Devadatta's followers plenty of food and other things they needed. When some of Buddha's followers heard about this, they told him and wished they could receive such generous support too.

The Blessed Lord then addressed them: "Do not yearn for gains, favors, and flattery from kings. While Prince Ajatasatru continues to support Devadatta in this way, Devadatta is destined for ruin, not spiritual growth. "Just as placing rotting liver on a rabid dog's nose would only intensify its madness, Prince Ajatasatru's support will lead to Devadatta's downfall. Such is the corrupting nature of excessive royal patronage and flattery.

"These are bitter obstacles that prevent true peace. Therefore, brethren, train yourselves thus: 'When gains, favors, and flattery come our way, we shall reject them. And if they do befall us, we shall not let them take hold of our hearts and make us servants of the prince.'"

If the King is Righteous His Subjects will be Righteous

Once the Lord, addressing the Almsmen, said: "When kings are unrighteous, their corruption spreads through their ministers to the Brahmins and householders, and finally reaches all townspeople and villagers. "Conversely, when kings are righteous, their virtue flows through all levels of society, from ministers to common folk." "Just as cattle crossing a river will follow when the lead bull swerves, so too will people follow when their leader strays from the right path. "Thus, the whole realm suffers when the king acts wrongly. But when cattle cross straight behind a true-coursed bull, so do people live righteously under a virtuous leader. When kings are good, the whole realm prospers in happiness."

The Duty of the Victor Who Has Won Peace

When victors win wars, they often claim the right to subjugate or enslave the defeated. The Buddha held a radically different view. He taught that true peace requires the victor to serve those they have conquered. Here are his words to the Bhikkhus on this matter: "After winning peace, the skilled warrior must demonstrate nobility—speaking graciously, showing kindness, and eschewing arrogance. They should be a considerate, grateful guest who maintains self-discipline and wisdom while avoiding meddling, boasting, or imposing their will. They must never descend into base or contemptible behavior worthy of reproach. "May all beings flourish in well-being and peace; may peace bless them always—every creature, whether mighty or humble, great or small, visible or invisible, near or far, born or yet to come—may peace embrace them all! "Let no one deceive or mock another; let none harbor thoughts of harm born of anger or hatred. "Just as a mother would shield her only child from harm with her own life, cultivate this all-encompassing love for every living being—an boundless love for all creation in its vastness, pure love untainted by hatred, stirring no enmity. "Whether standing, walking, sitting, or lying down, contemplate this truth with all your being: 'This is the divine state.'"

Chapter 20

Establishment of Buddhist Sanghs

Buddha's followers were divided into two main groups: monks (called bhikkhus) and regular followers (called upasakas). The monks were organized into a community called the Sangh, while regular followers remained outside this formal organization. The Buddhist monks emerged from a much older tradition of wandering spiritual seekers called parivrajakas, whose history predated Buddha himself. These wanderers had renounced their family lives to search for truth, traveling to meet different teachers and discuss fundamental questions about life, ethics, and the nature of reality. Both men and women could be wanderers, traveling either together or alone.

Buddha transformed this tradition significantly. While the earlier wanderers had no formal organization or rules, he created a structured community (the Sangh) with clear guidelines and purpose. The Sangh was remarkably egalitarian for its time—anyone could join regardless of social class, gender, or background. Within the community, members earned respect through their actions rather than their birth status. Buddha illustrated this concept with an elegant metaphor: the Sangh was like an ocean, and its members were like rivers. Just as rivers lose their individual identities when flowing into the ocean, those who joined the Sangh became part of one unified community, leaving behind their former social status. The only distinction maintained was between men and women, who had separate groups.

New members could join as either beginners (Shramaneras) or full monks (Bhikkhus). Those under twenty could become Shramaneras by pledging three basic promises: to follow Buddha, his teachings (Dhamma), and the community (Sangh). They also committed to *ten fundamental rules: "I will not kill; I will not steal; I will live a pure life; I will not lie; I will not drink alcohol; I will not eat at wrong times; I will avoid improper behavior; I will not wear decorations; I will live simply; I will not care about money.*" Shramaneras could return to secular life whenever they chose, and while learning from experienced monks, they weren't yet full members.

Becoming a full monk (Bhikkhu) required completing two stages: Parivraja and Upasampada. For Parivraja, one needed an experienced teacher (called an Uppadhya) with at least 10 years of monastic life. This teacher would guide the aspirant through training. Afterward, the teacher would present the candidate to the Sangh for Upasampada. The community would evaluate the candidate's readiness through questioning, and only upon approval would they become a Bhikkhu. Women followed similar steps to join the female monk community (Bhikkhuni Sangh).

The Bhikkhu and His Vows A Bhikkhu may possess only eight articles: - Three pieces of cloth to cover his body: (i) Lower garment (Antarvaska) (ii) Upper garment (Uttarasang) (iii) Covering garment for cold (Sanghati) - A girdle for the loins - An alms-bowl - A razor - A needle - A water-strainer.

A Bhikkhu takes the vow of poverty—living on alms, eating only one meal a day, and dwelling under a tree when no Vihar is available. Unlike other religious orders, Bhikkhus follow self-development rather than obedience to superiors. They must follow the Dhamma's teachings, as no superior has special powers of wisdom or forgiveness. Each monk is responsible for their own spiritual journey. Breaking vows leads to expulsion from the Sangh. Bhikkhus must also follow two sets of restrictions: The Nissagiya-Pacittiya has 26 rules about accepting gifts, handling money, and managing Sangh property. Breaking these requires restoration and repentance. Additionally, they must follow 92 Pacittiya restrictions.

Buddha's Conception of What a Bhikkhu Should Be

The Buddha himself told the Bhikkhus what he expected of them. Here are his words: "One who wishes to wear the yellow robe without having cleansed himself from sin, who disregards temperance and truth, is unworthy of the yellow robe. "But one who has cleansed himself from sin, is well grounded in all virtues, and endowed with temperance and truth—he is indeed worthy of the yellow robe.

"A man is not a mendicant (Bhikkhu) simply because he asks others for alms; he who adopts the whole law is a Bhikkhu, not he who merely begs. "He who rises above evil, who is chaste, who moves through the world with care—he indeed is called a Bhikkhu.

"Not by discipline and vows alone, not by much learning, not by entering into trance, not by sleeping alone do I earn the happiness of release which no worldling can know. O Bhikkhu, he who has extinguished desires has gained confidence.

"The Bhikkhu who controls his mouth, who speaks wisely and calmly, who teaches the meaning of the law—his word is sweet.

"He who dwells in the law, delights in the law, meditates on the law, reflects on the law—that Bhikkhu will never fall away from the true law.

"Let him not despise what he has received, nor envy others; a mendicant who envies others cannot find peace of mind.

"A Bhikkhu who, though receiving little, does not despise what he has received—even the gods will praise him if his life is pure and he is not slothful.

"He who never identifies himself with name and fórm, and does not grieve over what is no more—he indeed is called a Bhikkhu. "

The Bhikkhu who acts with kindness, who finds joy in Buddha's doctrine, will reach Nibbana—happiness arising from the cessation of natural inclinations.

"O Bhikkhu, empty this boat! When emptied, it will go quickly; having cut off passion and hatred, you will reach Nibbana.

"Cut off the five fetters, leave the five, rise above the five. A

Bhikkhu who has escaped from the five fetters is called Oghatinna—'saved from the flood.'

"Meditate, O Bhikkhu, and be not heedless! Do not direct your thoughts toward pleasure.

"Without knowledge there is no meditation, without meditation there is no knowledge; one who has both knowledge and meditation draws near to Nibbana.

"A Bhikkhu who has entered his empty house, whose mind is tranquil, experiences more than human delight when seeing the Dhamma clearly.

"And this is the beginning for a wise Bhikkhu: watchfulness over the senses, contentment, restraint under the Dhamma; keep noble friends whose lives are pure and who are not slothful.

"Let him live on charity, let him be perfect in his duties; then in the fullness of delight he will end all suffering.

"Rouse yourself by yourself, examine yourself by yourself; thus self-protected and attentive you will live happily, O Bhikkhu.

"For self is the lord of self, self is the refuge of self; therefore curb yourself as the merchant curbs a noble horse.

"A Bhikkhu who delights in earnestness, who fears thoughtlessness, moves about like fire, burning all fetters, small or large.

"A Bhikkhu who delights in reflection, who fears thoughtlessness, cannot fall from his perfect state—he is close to Nibbana.

The disciples of Gotama are always well awake, and their thoughts day and night dwell on Buddha.

The disciples of Gotama are always well awake, and their thoughts day and night dwell on the Dhamma.

The disciples of Gotama are always well awake, and their thoughts day and night dwell on their body.

The disciples of Gotama are always well awake, and their minds day and night delight in compassion.

The disciples of Gotama are always well awake, and their minds day and night delight in meditation.

It is hard to leave the world to become a friar, hard to enjoy the world; hard is the monastery life, painful are the houses; painful it is to dwell with equals, and the wandering mendicant faces many hardships.

A person full of faith, if endowed with virtue and glory, is respected wherever they may go.

The Bhikkhu and the Upasaka

Buddhism distinguishes between two main groups of followers: monks (Bhikkhus) and lay practitioners (Upasakas). While both adhere to Buddhism's core principles, their lifestyles and commitments differ. Monks lead a celibate, renunciant life, owning no possessions, maintaining no family ties, and adhering strictly to the ten precepts, including abstaining from hunting and certain dietary restrictions. Lay practitioners, while striving to follow the same precepts as guidelines, have greater flexibility in their daily lives, including marriage, family, and ownership of property.

. . .

The Buddha established the monastic community as a practical demonstration of Buddhist values in action, not merely as a theoretical concept. Monks dedicate themselves to personal spiritual development and assisting others. Their dual role involves self-cultivation and compassionate service, recognizing that true monastic practice necessitates both inner growth and actively alleviating the suffering of others. Renouncing worldly life allows monks to dedicate themselves fully to this purpose, not to escape from it.

While some criticize Buddhism as solely focused on monks, this is inaccurate. The Buddha's core teachings are universally applicable. In fact, they are particularly relevant to lay practitioners navigating the complexities of daily life. This is evidenced by the Buddha's own teachings, such as his discourse to Dhammika in Shravasti, which outlined specific guidelines for both monks and lay followers.

While the rules for *monks emphasize renunciation and spiritual discipline* (e.g., restricted food consumption, solitary meditation, spiritual discussions), those for *lay practitioners focus on ethical conduct* (e.g., non-violence, honesty, marital fidelity, abstaining from intoxicants), regular observance, supporting the monastic community, and fulfilling familial and professional responsibilities. Ultimately, while monks pursue complete liberation, lay practitioners aim for a more accessible form of spiritual progress within their circumstances. The fundamental principles of Buddhism, however, are intended for everyone, regardless of their path.

Principles for the Householder

One day, while Buddha was at a place called the Squirrels' Feeding-ground in Rajagaha, he met a young man named Sigala. Sigala was bowing in all six directions as part of his morning prayer. When Buddha asked him about this practice, Sigala simply said he was doing it because his dying father had asked him to. Buddha kindly offered to teach Sigala a more meaningful way to practice this ritual, and Sigala was happy to learn.

"A true religion must teach people to avoid harmful conduct. The four vices to shun are: taking life, stealing, sexual misconduct, and lying.

"Remember, Sigala, evil deeds spring from four sources: favoritism, hatred, foolishness, and fear. One who resists these impulses will not commit evil.

"A true religion must also teach the wise use of wealth. Six behaviors waste wealth: drinking intoxicants, wandering streets at inappropriate hours, excessive entertainment, gambling, keeping bad company, and laziness.

"Drinking intoxicants brings six dangers: loss of wealth, increased conflict, poor health, damaged reputation, shameful behavior, and weakened mental clarity.

"Roaming streets at inappropriate hours brings six perils: leaving yourself and family unprotected, exposing your property to theft, arousing suspicion, attracting false rumors, and inviting trouble.

"Excessive entertainment leads to endless pursuit of dancing, singing, music, performances, and revelry.

"Gambling brings six perils: victory creates enemies, loss brings sorrow, wealth disappears, your word loses value, friends and officials scorn you, and no one will marry you—for who trusts a gambler to support a family? "Bad companions bring six perils: you'll befriend gamblers, hedonists, drunkards, cheats, swindlers, and violent people.

"Laziness brings six perils: claiming it's too cold, too hot, too early, too late, too hungry, or too full to work. While duties go unfulfilled, new wealth vanishes and old wealth fades.

"Beware four types of false friends: the taker, the empty talker, the flatterer, and the wastrel. The taker is false because he takes much, gives little, acts from fear, and serves only himself. The empty talker is false because he speaks of past and future friendship, offers hollow words, and claims helplessness when needed. The flatterer is false because he encourages wrong and discourages right, praising you present but slandering you absent. The wastrel is false because he joins you in late-night wandering, excessive entertainment, and gambling."

"Four friends prove true-hearted: the helper, the steadfast friend, the counselor, and the sympathizer. The helper proves true by guarding you when vulnerable, protecting your property, offering refuge in times of fear, and providing double what you need in times of necessity. The steadfast friend proves true by sharing secrets with you, keeping your confidences, standing beside you in trouble, and offering their life for you. The counselor proves true by restraining you from wrong, encouraging right action, sharing wisdom, and showing the path to understanding. The sympathizer proves true by finding no joy in your misfortunes, delighting in your success, silencing those who speak ill of you, and supporting those who praise you."

"Rather than teaching mere worship of the six directions, a true religion must teach respect and reverence for parents, teachers, family, friends, workers, and spiritual guides."

Chapter 21

Buddha's Critics

The Buddha, despite his enlightenment and teachings of compassion, faced significant opposition. This highlights a universal truth: even the most virtuous individuals can attract negativity. The Buddha challenged existing religious and social norms, naturally leading to resistance from those who felt threatened. His teachings, like any complex philosophy, was misinterpreted & criticised based on flawed assumptions. The Buddha's growing influence and the devotion he inspired triggered lot of negative emotions in others. Here we'll see some of those instances.

Accusations of Converting People Through Charisma

One day at the Great Wood in Vesali, a man named Bhaddiya came to Buddha with a concern. People were saying Buddha used his charm to convert followers. Buddha's response was simple and wise - he taught Bhaddiya how to think carefully about what to believe. Buddha explained that people shouldn't automatically believe something just because: Someone else told them about it It's an old tradition It's written in religious texts It sounds like it makes sense It fits with what they already believe The person telling them is someone they respect and has charm. As they talked, Buddha explained that he didn't use any special tricks. His only method was teaching people how to overcome three basic problems: greed, anger, and confusion. Bhaddiya liked this honest approach so much that he hoped everyone, no matter their social status, could learn these teachings.

Charge of Being a Dependant Parasite!

A man once accused Buddha of being lazy and living off other people's work. One morning, Buddha went to a village where a farmer named Kasi-Bharadvaja was getting ready to plant his crops. Like other monks, Buddha carried a bowl to collect food offerings. When the farmer saw Buddha, he said, "Hey! I have to work hard in my fields before I can eat. You should do the same!"

Buddha answered, "I do work before I eat, just like you."

The farmer looked at Buddha and said, "Really? I don't see any farming tools with you. Where's your plow? Where are your oxen? How can you say you work?"

Buddha smiled and explained with a simple comparison: "I'm a different kind of farmer. My faith is like a seed, my self-discipline is like rain, and wisdom is my plow. Being careful about my actions is like a farming tool, and staying mindful helps guide me. I'm careful about what I say and do. I eat just what I need. I remove bad thoughts like you remove weeds from your field. I work hard toward finding peace, just like a strong ox that never stops. What I'm growing is understanding, and anyone who farms this way can find freedom from life's troubles."

The farmer was amazed by this answer. He offered Buddha some milk-rice, saying, "Please eat - you really are a farmer, growing wisdom instead of crops!"

But Buddha kindly refused, saying, "I don't take payment for teaching - that's not what we do. Please give this food to someone else who needs it. That's how you'll earn good karma." These words touched the farmer's heart. He bowed to Buddha and said Buddha had helped him see the truth, like bringing light into darkness. The farmer was so moved that he asked to become Buddha's student, and Buddha welcomed him.

Charge of Breaking Happy Households

People started complaining when many young nobles from Magadha began following Buddha. They said, "Buddha is breaking up families by taking sons away from their parents and husbands from their wives!"

These complaints grew louder because Buddha had recently gained many new followers: 1,000 holy men called Jatilas, 250 students of a teacher named Sanjaya, and many well-known young men from Magadha. The townspeople were worried about who might join him next.

When Buddha's monks walked through town, people would shout at them: "Look! The great Buddha has come to our city and taken all of Sanjaya's followers. Who's next?"

When the monks told Buddha about these complaints, he stayed calm and said, "Don't worry. These complaints will only last seven days before they stop."

He then taught his monks how to answer these critics: "Tell them that good teachers like me guide people through teaching, not by forcing them. How can anyone fairly criticize wisdom? What's wrong with teaching people what's right? Remember to tell them that no one is forced to follow my teachings - everyone is free to choose whether to become a monk or live a normal life."

Once the monks started explaining things this way, people began to understand. They realized, "Buddha actually leads people through good teachings, not by tricking them." After this, the complaints stopped.

False Charge of Murder

A religious group called the Tirthikas started losing followers after Buddha became popular. Many people had never even heard of them. Jealous and desperate, they made an evil plan. They asked a woman named Sundari to help them hurt Buddha's reputation. "You're beautiful, Sundari," they said. "People will believe you if you spread lies about Buddha."

Following their plan, Sundari would walk to Buddha's garden temple every evening with flowers and perfume. When anyone asked where she was going, she would say, "I'm going to spend the night with Buddha."

But this was a lie. She actually spent her nights in the Tirthikas' gardens. In the mornings, she would falsely tell people she had been with Buddha.

Then the Tirthikas went even further with their plan. They paid some men to kill Sundari and leave her body near Buddha's temple. After the murder, they went to the police and reported Sundari missing, mentioning that she often visited Buddha's temple.

When her body was found, the Tirthikas blamed Buddha's followers, saying they had killed her to hide a scandal. But their plan failed when the killers started fighting in a bar about how to split the money they were paid for the murder.

The police arrested them, and they admitted everything, including how the Tirthikas had planned it all. After this was revealed, the Tirthikas lost all their remaining respect among the people.

False Charge of Immorality

The Tirthikas, Getting desperate, they tried standing in the streets calling out: "We're just as enlightened as Buddha! Give us donations - it'll bring you just as much good luck as giving to him!" But people just ignored them.

So they came up with a plan to hurt Buddha's reputation. They found a beautiful woman named Chincha and asked her to help them spread false stories about Buddha.

Chincha agreed to help. Every evening, she would dress up nicely and walk toward Buddha's monastery carrying flowers and perfumes. When anyone asked where she was going, she would rudely say it wasn't their business.

Though she actually spent her nights at the Tirthikas' place near the monastery, she told people the next morning that she had spent the night with Buddha. This made some people start to doubt Buddha.

Four months later, she started padding her clothes to make herself look pregnant. She told everyone Buddha was responsible. Some people believed her.

When she appeared to be nine months pregnant (using a wooden bump tied to her belly), she went to where Buddha was teaching. In front of everyone, she accused him: "You teach others about doing good, but you got me pregnant and won't even help me prepare for the baby!"

While everyone watched in silence, Buddha simply said, "Sister, only you and I know what's really true."

Chincha confidently replied, "Yes, that's right!" But just then, she coughed, and the rope holding her fake pregnancy bump came loose. The wooden bump fell to the ground in front of everyone, showing that she had been lying all along.

When people saw that she had tried to trick them, they chased her away.

Devadatta - The evil cousin

Devadatta was Buddha's cousin, but he was very jealous of Buddha and often acted against him.

After Buddha left his palace life, Devadatta did something wrong - he tried to win over Buddha's wife, Yeshodhara. He dressed as a monk and snuck into her room one night. When she thought he might have news from Buddha, Devadatta instead tried to seduce her. When that failed, he tried to make her angry at her husband.

"He doesn't care about you. He just left you behind," Devadatta said. But Yeshodhara stood up for Buddha, saying, "He left to help many people end their suffering. Never show your face again in this kingdom! "

Later, Devadatta got very jealous that he tried to kill Buddha three different times:

First, he rolled a big rock down a hill when Buddha was walking below. The rock missed, but a small piece hurt Buddha's foot. Second, he got Prince Ajata-satru to send someone to kill Buddha. But when the time came, the person couldn't do it. Third, he paid people to let loose a dangerous elephant named Nalagiri when Buddha was walking by. This plan didn't work either.

After all these failed attempts, Devadatta lost everything. The king stopped helping him, and he had to beg for food. When he went to another kingdom hoping for help, King Prasenjit turned him away.

Why the Buddha didnt write books

The Buddha taught for 45 years, but he never wrote down his teachings. Instead, he focused on teaching the dhamma - important life principles that went beyond just written words. To understand Buddhism, people need to do three things: listen to the teachings, think deeply about them, and put them into practice. At its core, Buddhism is about living a good life through proper behavior, meditation, and gaining wisdom from direct experience. The goal is to reach a deep understanding, like the Buddha did.

. . .

There's a good reason why these teachings weren't written down at first. Like learning to play music, understanding Buddhism requires hands-on practice with a teacher - not just reading about it. In ancient India, teachers passed down knowledge by speaking it to their students. This was true even for ancient texts like the Vedas. This direct teaching from person to person created an unbroken chain of knowledge from the Buddha to today's Buddhist monks (the Sangha). To become a monk, you need five experienced monks present - this helps maintain this connection to the original teachings.

While anyone can learn Buddhist teachings, the monks have played a crucial role in preserving and sharing these lessons throughout history. Buddhism teaches people how to free themselves from suffering by letting go of wants, training their minds, and living ethically. This includes being mindful of your thoughts, words, and actions, and building mental strength through meditation. Next, we'll look at specific meditation practices from early Buddhist texts, focusing on the Theravada tradition.

Chapter 22

The Buddha's Last days

The Buddha continued his missionary work even after appointing other missionaries. He established main centers at Shravasti and Rajagraha, visiting them 75 and 24 times respectively. His minor centers included Kapilavastu, Vesali, and Kamas-sadhamma. His travels extended across Northern India, covering vast distances on foot. He visited numerous places including Ukkatha, Nalanda, Kushinara, and many others across the Sakya, Kuru and Anga regions. The distance between places was significant - for example, Rajagraha was 250 miles from Lumbini. Living simply with three pieces of clothing and one meal a day, he stayed mostly under trees until his disciples built resting places. He traveled from village to village, teaching and addressing doubts. Despite many challenges, he cheerfully continued his mission of spreading the dharma.

Before their deaths, Mahaprajapati and Yeshodhara met the Blessed Lord for their final meeting. Mahaprajapati approached first and worshipped him. She expressed gratitude for the happiness his teachings had brought her—for being spiritually reborn through him, for the doctrine growing within her, for having nursed him with the Dhamma-milk, and for helping her cross the ocean of becoming. "What a glorious thing it has been to be known as the mother of the Buddha!" she exclaimed. Then she made her plea: "I desire to die finally, having put away this corpse. O sorrow-ender, permit me."

Yeshodhara then addressed the Blessed Lord, telling him she was in her seventy-eighth year. The Blessed Lord replied that he was in his eighties. She informed him that she would die that very night. Unlike Mahaprajapati, her tone was more self-reliant—she neither asked permission to die nor sought him as her refuge. Instead, she declared to him (me saranam atthano), "I am my own refuge." Having conquered all the impurities in her life, she came simply to thank him for showing her the way and giving her the power.

Once when the Lord was staying at Raja-graha in the bamboo grove, Rahula was staying at Ambalathika. The Blessed One, arising from his meditation in the evening, went to visit Rahula. Seeing the Lord approaching from afar, Rahula prepared a seat and water to wash his feet. After Buddha sat down he addressed Rahula:

"One who tells deliberate lies has—I say—left no evil deed undone. Therefore, you must train yourself never to tell a lie, even in jest.

Apply this reflection to every act you perform, every word you speak, and every thought you think.

Before taking any action, reflect whether it would harm yourself or others or both. Such harmful acts produce suffering and lead to more suffering. If your reflection reveals this nature in your intended action, do not do it.

But if your reflection shows the act brings no harm and only good, then you may proceed.

Cultivate loving kindness, and malevolence will fade away.

Cultivate compassion, and vexation will fade away.

Cultivate joy in others' well-being, and aversions will fade away.

Cultivate balanced equanimity, and all repugnance will fade away.

Cultivate awareness of the body's impermanence, and passion will fade away.

Cultivate understanding of life's transient nature, and the pride of self will fall away."

Glad at heart, Rahula rejoiced in what the Lord had said.

At the Jetavana monastery in Shravasti, Sariputta came to see Buddha with 500 of his followers. He told Buddha that he was ready to die and asked for permission to spend his final moments in his hometown, Nalaka village. In a touching moment, Sariputta knelt at Buddha's feet and thanked him, saying he was happy to have achieved everything he had wanted in life. Buddha asked the assembly to follow Sariputta as he left, making it an emotional goodbye for everyone. Later, Sariputta died peacefully in the house where he grew up.

When his followers brought Sariputta's ashes, Buddha spoke beautiful words about him: "Sariputta was our wisest teacher. He lived without greed and worked hard to help others. He stayed away from wrongdoing - these ashes are all that remain of him. He was as patient as the earth itself. He never got angry and wasn't controlled by desires. He had overcome all negative feelings and showed true kindness, friendship, and love to everyone."

Soon after this, Buddha faced another loss when his other main student, Mahamogallana, was killed by attackers near Rajagraha. Losing both of his closest disciples - who were known as the Defenders of the Faith - made Buddha very sad, and he decided to leave Shravasti.

As Buddha grew older, he needed someone to help take care of him. He chose Ananda, who became not just his assistant but his closest friend until the end of his life. When Buddha reached Kushinara, he rested between two Sal trees. Feeling that his death was near, He called Ananda and said, "Tonight, during the third watch of the night, I will pass away here in Kushinara, between these twin Sal trees."

Ananda was deeply saddened and begged Buddha, "Please, Lord, stay with us longer for the happiness of all people and for the good of the world." Buddha gently refused, saying, "No more, Ananda. The time for such requests has passed. I am now eighty years old and my life is coming to an end. Like an old cart that finally breaks down, my body must now give way."

Hearing this, Ananda left the place, overcome with grief. When Buddha noticed Ananda was gone, he asked where he was. Others told him that Ananda had left to cry.

Buddha sent someone to bring him back. When Ananda returned, Buddha comforted him: "Don't cry, Ananda. Haven't I always said that we must eventually part from everything and everyone we love?"

He praised Ananda, saying, "You have served me with great kindness and love. Keep working hard on your spiritual path, and you too will free yourself from all suffering."

Speaking to the other monks, Buddha praised Ananda's wisdom and said that everyone felt happy around him. He mentioned four special qualities about Ananda: people were always happy to visit him, to see him, to hear him speak, and they felt uncomfortable when he was quiet.

Ananda and Anurudha spent the rest of the night discussing Buddha's teachings. Later that night, just as he had said, Buddha passed away peacefully.

When Buddha died, Ananda and the other monks were overwhelmed with sadness.

They wept and some even fell to the ground in grief, crying out, "The Buddha has left us too soon! The light of the world has gone out!"

Buddha died at midnight on the full moon day of Vaishakha in the year 483 BCE.

As the Pali text says:

Diva tapati addicco Ratin abhati candima;

Sannaddho khathio tapati Jhayi tapati brahamano;

Atha Sabbain ahorattain Buddho tapati tejasa.

"The sun shines only in the day and the moon brightens the night. The warrior shines in his armor, and the Brahmin shines in meditation. But the Buddha shines over all, day and night, by his own glory. He was, beyond question, the light of the world."

Chapter 23

Basic principles of Buddhist meditation

So far we have read about what constitutes The Dhamma. The practise of Dhamma is Meditation. Let me make an audacious statement. The way out of every addiction is meditation. *(Think about it, we can debate later)*

Buddhism teaches that our minds are naturally pure and clear, like clean water. However, just as water can become cloudy with dirt, our minds can become clouded by negative thoughts and emotions. These negative influences are temporary—they're not a permanent part of who we are. "Radiant is the mind, monks, but sometimes it is defiled by defilements that come from without. The ordinary person without understanding does not know it as it truly is."

The main goal of Buddhist practice is to clear the mind of these negative influences. Think of your mind as a clear pool of water that sometimes gets murky. Buddhist meditation helps restore the mind to its natural, clear state. This clarity helps us understand ourselves better and see reality as it truly is.

There are two main types of meditation that work together:

1. Calm meditation—which helps us quiet disturbing thoughts temporarily

2. Insight meditation—which, when combined with calm meditation, can permanently remove these disturbing thoughts

Buddhist meditation teaches us to look inside ourselves to better understand how our minds work. However, five main challenges can get in our way:

- Wanting pleasurable things (craving and greed)

- Feeling angry or frustrated when meditation results don't meet our expectations

- Feeling too tired, lazy, or sleepy to meditate

- Being either too excited or feeling too down at initial stages of meditation

- Having doubts about whether the practice is worthwhile

Just as you can't see your reflection clearly in disturbed water, these mental challenges prevent us from seeing our true nature. But when our mind is free from these challenges—like still, clear water—we can see the truth without any distortion. This is the basic theory of Buddhist meditation, as taught by The Master Buddhaghosa.

Chapter 24
Calm Meditation

Stilling the mind

Calm Meditation Calm meditation techniques train the mind to focus on a single object rather than constantly seeking new sensations. This develops concentration (samādhi), which allows the mind to rest peacefully on one point of focus. Through practice, the mind reaches a state of joy & deep contentment with its chosen object.

In this meditative state (called samādhi or dhyāna), awareness shifts beyond ordinary sensory experiences into a refined consciousness that perceives pure mental forms.

Calm meditation begins with choosing a suitable meditation object. These objects fall into two categories: 1. Objects suited for different stages of practice 2. Objects matched to different personality types.

For beginners, meditation can focus on any of the objects mentioned below. Meditators can concentrate on a single aspect of Buddha's Dhamma teachings, such as meditating on developing good conduct, generosity, compassion, or mindfulness of death during their calm meditation session. This single-pointed focus on one object or virtue helps achieve progressively deeper states of joy and develop "access concentration."

The levels progress as Access concentration —> Increasing stages of Jhana. Then, depending on the Jhana level, suitable objects can be chosen for meditation. The ten devices (kasina) and breath meditations work for both beginners and advanced practitioners, while formless meditations are reserved for advanced practice only.

Below you'll find a table that shows which meditation objects work best for different people and different skill levels. The table uses colors to make it easier to understand which types of meditation are recommended for beginners versus more experienced meditators.

Meditation subjects are matched to personality types. Those with strong sexual desires / excessive material comfort & greed practice "ugliness" meditations on 10 stages of bodily decay.

The religious types benefit from recollections, overthinkers / anxious types benefit from breath meditation, and the short tempered from 4 colored disc meditation.

Category	Subject	Personality Suitability	Level Achieved
10 Kasinas (Devices)	Earth	All personality types	1st-4th Jhana
	Water	All personality types	1st-4th Jhana
	Fire	All personality types	1st-4th Jhana
	Air	All personality types	1st-4th Jhana
	Blue		1st-4th Jhana
	Yellow		1st-4th Jhana
	Red	Hate	1st-4th Jhana
	White		1st-4th Jhana
	Light	All personality types	1st-4th Jhana
	Limited Space	All personality types	1st-4th Jhana
10 Asubhas (Repulsions)	The bloated (corpse)	Greed	1st Jhana
	The livid (corpse)	Greed	1st Jhana
	The festering (corpse)	Greed	1st Jhana
	The cut-up (corpse)	Greed	1st Jhana
	The gnawed (corpse)	Greed	1st Jhana
	The scattered (corpse)	Greed	1st Jhana
	The hacked and scattered (corpse)	Greed	1st Jhana
	The bleeding (corpse)	Greed	1st Jhana
	The worm-infested (corpse)	Greed	1st Jhana
	The skeleton (corpse)	Greed	1st Jhana
Miscellaneous	Repulsiveness of Food	Intelligent	Access Concentration
	Determining the 4 Elements	Intelligent	Access Concentration
10 Anussatis (Recollections)	Recollection of the Buddha	Faith	Access Concentration
	Recollection of the Dharma	Faith	Access Concentration
	Recollection of the Sangha	Faith	Access Concentration
	Recollection of Good Conduct	Faith	Access Concentration
	Recollection of Generosity	Faith	Access Concentration
	Recollection of the Gods	Faith	Access Concentration
	Mindfulness of Death	Intelligent/Greed	Access Concentration
	Mindfulness of the Body	Intelligent	1st Jhana
	Mindfulness of Breathing	Delusion/Distracted	1st-4th Jhana
	Mindfulness of Peace	Intelligent	Access Concentration
4 Appamaññas (Immeasurables)	Loving-kindness		1st-3rd Jhana
	Compassion		1st-3rd Jhana
	Sympathetic Joy	Hate	1st-3rd Jhana
	Equanimity		4th Jhana
4 Arupayatanas (Formless Meditations)	Boundless Space	All personality types	4th Jhana
	Boundless Consciousness	All personality types	4th Jhana
	Nothingness	All personality types	4th Jhana
	Neither Perception nor Non-Percep	All personality types	4th Jhana

Having a meditation teacher is very important. They can help you choose the right type of meditation and show you how to practice it correctly. Just like the Buddha's students trusted his guidance, you need to trust your meditation teacher. This trust helps you follow their instructions properly. Showing respect to your teacher, like bowing, can help build this trust.

Starting Meditation & common challenges

Starting meditation is actually quite simple. Find a quiet spot, sit cross-legged, with full lotus position / half lotus position or on a chair and focus your mind on whatever you've chosen to meditate on (like your breath). Your mind will naturally wander - when this happens, just *gently & lovingly* bring your attention back to your meditation focus. People often struggle with meditation for two main reasons: they get distracted by common problems (like sleepiness or restlessness), or they haven't yet developed enough practice with focusing their mind.

Learning to meditate is similar to learning any new skill. You'll face some common challenges: Getting distracted by more high pleasure activities (like watching TV or browsing your phone), Feeling annoyed by distractions or getting frustrated with your progress, Feeling tired during practice time, even if you're usually energetic, Having mood swings - sometimes feeling too excited, other times feeling discouraged, Questioning whether meditation is worth your time and effort.

Don't worry - these challenges are completely normal, and everyone faces them when learning to meditate. Think about learning to play an instrument, like a guitar. At first, you need to focus carefully on the basics - where to put your fingers and how to make each note sound right.

Similarly, when you start meditating, you need to pay attention to two things: your main focus point (like your breathing) and how well you're staying focused. Something wonderful happens as you keep practicing.

You start to enjoy the process more, and it feels more natural. This brings two positive changes: you feel joyful and happy while meditating. When you're enjoying yourself, it becomes easier to stay focused.

Eventually, you reach a state of deep concentration where your mind stays perfectly calm and focused on just one thing, without getting distracted. The stages of dhyana Meditation deepens gradually, like advancing through levels. You begin with the first level of deep concentration (dhyana) and progress upward.

The above manual presents a concise version of Buddhaghosa's stages of calm meditation. You can refer to other detailed books (Bibliography) to learn more about various forms of meditation. Progression in meditation requires intense practice. It's impossible to assess our own progress without guidance, which is why learning with a teacher is essential for serious practitioners.

The breakthrough from access concentration to 1st Jhana is particularly challenging. Some people spend their entire lives at the access concentration stage—which itself creates a far better mental state than a non-meditating mind.

Most Jhana states take decades to achieve, even with monastic discipline. Calm meditation is extremely effective and invaluable in relieving mental suffering, as supported by modern neuroscience. Think of it as giving your brain a warm bath—you can feel the elevated sense of joy that comes from turning inward. This practice can be done anytime, anywhere, like taking ***"meditation snacks"*** throughout the day.

During our everyday activities, whenever we notice our awareness wandering into unhealthy states like anger, greed, or ignorance, we gently & lovingly bring our attention back to our chosen meditative object. Consistent practice with calm meditation will infuse your life with positive joy that surpasses any sensual pleasures—without their accompanying regret.

This is the form of meditation we recommend that every human being should practice. It is a privilege to meditate, as no other life forms on Earth can do so. To demonstrate this gratitude, A practice is known as "Cow Meditation" is taught in Tibetan Buddhist traditions. Imagine yourself as a cow: visualize being bound in chains, standing in your own excrement, with flies buzzing all around. Picture having a pierced nose ring, being packed so tightly with other cows that you cannot move, having your milk extracted, and ultimately facing slaughter. Fully embody the cow's experience. Then, gently bring your awareness back to your present state as a human being. What a privilege this is. Does your current life situation truly warrant the unhealthy mental states we often indulge in?

Chapter 25
Insight meditation

Unless you're well experienced with calm meditation, you cannot experience the full benefits of insight meditation. The prerequisite for insight meditation is the ability to calm the mind at will. After achieving a calm and peaceful mind through meditation, particularly at a level of deep concentration (dhyana), the meditator can then focus on developing wisdom and understanding through insight meditation. The goal of insight meditation is to understand three basic truths about everything in life:

1. Impermanence: Everything is in a constant state of flux. Inner Thoughts, feelings, sensations, as well as the external world are always changing. This understanding can lead to less attachment and greater acceptance of life's ups and downs.

2. Interconnectedness: We are not isolated individuals but are deeply connected to everything around us. This realization can foster compassion and a sense of belonging to something larger than ourselves.

3. Suffering is a part of life: Suffering is inevitable, but we can learn to relate to it differently. By observing our experiences with mindfulness, we can develop a greater understanding of the nature of suffering and find ways to alleviate it.

It's important to note that these are just a few of the many insights that can arise from insight meditation. The practice is a journey of self-discovery, and each person's experience will be unique.

While different Buddhist schools may interpret these ideas in their own ways, all advanced Buddhist practices share the same goal: to directly experience and understand these three aspects of reality. Buddhist teachers have different views on when a meditator should start practicing insight meditation.

Some traditional teachers, like Upatissa, Buddhaghosa, and Vasubandhu, suggest two possible approaches:

- First develop deep states of calm meditation, then move on to insight meditation

- Start working on insight with just a basic foundation of calm

Different Buddhist traditions have their own ways of describing the stages of meditation. In the Theravada tradition, following the teacher Buddhaghosa, they use a system of stepwise "purifications".

The Steps of Purification by Buddhaghosha

Buddhism teaches that there are seven steps to spiritual growth.

The first two steps are straightforward: developing good behavior and learning to meditate calmly. These create a strong foundation for the deeper work that follows.

The third step is about changing how we see ourselves. Instead of thinking we have a fixed, unchanging self, we start to notice that we're made up of different parts that work together—our feelings, thoughts, and physical sensations. It's like two haystacks leaning on each other—they only stand up together. This shows how our mind and body need each other.

The fourth step helps us overcome our doubts. After we understand how our mind and body work together in the present moment, we start to see how everything is connected across time. This is called "dependent arising"—it means that nothing exists completely by itself. Everything comes from something else, like a long chain of causes and effects. There's no supreme being making things happen; instead, things naturally arise from other things. When someone deeply understands this through experience, it transforms their worldview. This insight removes doubts about Buddhist teachings, making them a "lesser stream-enterer." Through deep meditation, they perceive the world's impermanence.

Buddhaghosa illustrated this with simple & beautiful metaphors: Like morning dewdrops vanishing, Like water bubbles bursting, Like lightning flashing, Like a desert mirage In this state, they experience clarity, understanding, joy, focus, determination, alertness, and balance. However, they might become attached to these positive experiences, mistaking them for enlightenment until life's challenges reveal otherwise. Eventually, they return to simple observation, finding joy in seeing life's impermanent nature.

A simple story illustrates the stages of spiritual understanding: A fisherman caught what appeared to be a fish but discovered it was actually a snake. His journey mirrors Buddhist progress: initial joy at his catch (representing our attachment to self); fear upon discovering the snake's three marks (recognizing impermanence, suffering, and non-self) and realizing his pursuit was in vain; understanding the danger of holding onto the snake (representing self-identity, ego, and the human nature of greed, hatred, and ignorance); experiencing discomfort with this reality while feeling uncertain; desiring to let go of his attachment to the snake (the self); seeking freedom (through Buddha's teachings and Dhamma practice); carefully releasing the snake to ensure it doesn't return; and finally finding peace. This parallels the stages of meditation: initial contentment with our perceived self, progressive encounters with life's suffering as we mature, and recognizing the three truths of existence (suffering stems from unhealthy attachments, nothing is permanent, everything follows cause and effect). Then comes understanding the challenge (that virtuous practice and training the mind through meditation is the way out of suffering), experiencing discomfort with the practice, releasing attachments, seeking liberation, letting go, and finally achieving clarity.

This moment of understanding is called revealing of 'the path'—it unifies all previous meditation practice. Immediately following this insight comes a moment of profound peace, called the 'fruit.'

When reaching a deep meditative state, the mind progresses through various levels of concentration. At the level of "transcendent concentration," a remarkable transformation occurs. While ordinary meditation temporarily quiets negative thoughts and feelings, this transcendent state eliminates them permanently. This profound shift transforms an ordinary person into what Buddhists call a "noble one"—someone who has directly realized the basic truths about suffering,

The ten fetters which prevent us from the path of meditation

In ancient Buddhist texts, the ten fetters are mental chains that bind individuals to the cycle of suffering and rebirth (samsara). These fetters are obstacles to enlightenment and must be gradually eliminated to achieve liberation. The ten fetters are:

1. Belief in a self (Pali: sakkāya-diṭṭhi): The mistaken view that there is a permanent, unchanging self or soul.

2. Doubt or uncertainty (vicikicchā): Especially about the Buddha's awakening and teachings.

3. Attachment to rites and rituals (sīlabbata-parāmāsa): Clinging to rituals and practices without understanding their true meaning.

4. Sensual desire (kāmacchando): Craving for sensual pleasures and experiences.

5. Ill will (vyāpādo or byāpādo): Negative emotions such as anger, hatred, and resentment.

6. Lust for material existence (rūparāgo):Desire for rebirth in the material realm.

7. Lust for immaterial existence (arūparāgo):Desire for rebirth in the formless realm.

8. Conceit (māna): Pride, arrogance, and a sense of superiority.

9. Restlessness (uddhacca):Mental agitation and inability to find peace.

10. Ignorance (avijjā): Lack of understanding of the true nature of reality and the Four Noble Truths.

The ten fetters are gradually abandoned as one progresses along the Buddhist path, beginning with the first three at stream-entry and culminating in complete liberation.

This progression happens through four stages:

1. "Stream-enterer": Eliminates the first three fetters

2. "Once-returner": Eliminates the first three fetters and weakens the next two

3. "Non-returner": Eliminates the five lower fetters

4. "Arhat": Eliminates all ten fetters, achieving complete enlightenment without rebirth

The earliest Buddhist texts present two possible ways these stages unfold:

1. One may reach any of the four stages directly, based on their circumstances

2. One must progress through each stage sequentially, either in one lifetime or across multiple lives

Later Buddhist teachers interpreted this differently. Buddhaghosa believed people typically progress through the stages sequentially, though sometimes rapidly. Vasubandhu, however, taught that people could attain any stage directly.

The Five Paths to Enlightenment

According to ancient Buddhist teachers Vasubandhu and Asanga, there are five main paths to spiritual awakening:

1. The Path of Preparation: This is the foundation of spiritual life, focusing on developing faith, generosity, good behavior, and basic meditation skills (both calming and insight practices).

2. The Path of Practice: Here, you deepen your meditation skills, especially insight meditation.

3. The Path of Seeing: In this path, you directly experience the truths that Buddha taught.

4. The Path of Development: Mastering deep meditation states & Learning to let go of attachment to everything, including these meditation experiences themselves

5. The Path of Completion: This is the final stage where you become fully enlightened (an arhat).

The journey typically begins with calm meditation. You might: Focus on the unattractive aspects of things, Practice mindful breathing & Develop concentration.

Then you move to the "four foundations of mindfulness," where you observe: Your body, Your feelings (pleasant, unpleasant, or neutral), Your mind & All physical and mental experiences together.

As you practice, your understanding deepens through several stages. These stages help you understand the four noble truths more deeply.

The final breakthrough happens in a very short time - like a flash of insight. This leads to permanent positive changes in your mind. Your progress depends on your previous meditation experience: If you're already skilled in deep meditation, you might quickly become a once-returner or never-returner (advanced spiritual stages). If you're newer to meditation, you'll start as a stream-enterer (first stage) and gradually progress through the stages.

Either way, the final goal is becoming an arhat - someone who has completely freed themselves from all mental obstacles and reached full enlightenment.

Paradoxically, many modern schools of Buddhism have done away with the concept of enlightenment completely.

All these different stages and levels might seem complicated and overwhelming. But they're really just trying to explain something simple: ***spiritual growth happens gradually, through consistent practice***. It's like building a skill - you keep doing the same basic exercise over and over, watching how things come and go in the world around you and how they're all connected.

While this growth is gradual, you'll notice certain milestones along the way. And at some point, you'll have a sudden "aha moment" that changes how you see everything. This deep understanding permanently changes who you are. Here's a simple story that explains this better than any list of stages could: Think of a craftsman working with a chisel. Each day, he holds the chisel and works with it, but he doesn't notice how the handle is slowly wearing down from use. He can't tell how much wore away today, or yesterday, or last week. But when the handle is completely worn down, he suddenly notices the change. This is exactly like meditation practice.

The person meditating doesn't notice their negative thoughts and habits wearing away day by day. But when these habits are finally gone, they suddenly realize how much they've changed.

Calm (Samatha) Meditation Vs Insight (Vipassana) Meditations

These two types of meditation actually help each other. To see those three truths clearly, we need a calm mind. And to truly let go of our deepest attachments, we need to experience very peaceful states of meditation and then understand that even these don't last forever. This is why most people practice both types. Modern Buddhist teachers sometimes disagree about which type is more important. Some Western teachers focus more on insight meditation. They say that since even the deepest peaceful states don't last, we shouldn't worry too much about reaching them. Instead, they suggest working on insight from the beginning. Most agree that both calm and insight are valuable - they're just different tools for the same goal. The most important thing to remember is that these aren't opposing practices. They're complementary ways to develop wisdom and peace of mind. Whether you practice in a traditional way or follow a simpler modern approach, both types of meditation can help you grow spiritually.

Integrating Both Practices

In many traditions, calm and insight meditations are practiced together. For example:

- Calm meditation is often used as a foundation to stabilize the mind before engaging in insight meditation

- The deep concentration developed in calm meditation can enhance the clarity and precision of insight practices.

- Conversely, insights gained through Vipassana can deepen the understanding of the states achieved in Samatha.

Practical Example

- Calm Meditation: Sit and focus solely on the breath. If the mind wanders, gently bring it back to the breath. The goal is to achieve a state of deep calm and stillness.

- Insight Meditation: After calming the mind, observe the breath and then expand your awareness to include bodily sensations, thoughts, and emotions. Notice how these phenomena arise and pass away, reflecting on their impermanent and selfless nature.

Chapter 26

Buddhism as a worldwide religion

After the Buddha's passing, his disciples spread his teachings far and wide to alleviate human suffering. As these teachings traveled through different places and times, they combined with local cultural beliefs and practices, giving rise to multiple schools of Buddhism. While we will explore some of these schools, remember: "*Though the paths may vary, the starting point is always suffering, and the destination is freedom from suffering*"

Southern Buddhism : Theravada Buddhism (Sri Lanka, South East Asia)

Buddhism arrived in Sri Lanka around 250 BCE, becoming a key center for Theravada Buddhism. This tradition was preserved through monastic rules (Vinaya) and sacred texts at the Mahavihara monastery, taking its final form by 1000 CE.

The city of Anuradhapura had three major monasteries:

- Mahavihara (250 BCE)

- Abhayagiri (100 BCE)

- Jetavana (300 CE)

In the 400s CE, scholars Buddhaghosa and Buddhadatta organized Buddhist teachings into three collections:

1. The Vinaya Pitaka - monastic rules

2. The Sutta Pitaka - Buddha's teachings

3. The Abhidhamma Pitaka - doctrinal explanations

Sri Lankan Buddhism faced challenges after South Indian conquest in 1215 and subsequent European colonization. The tradition survived through Southeast Asian support and royal patronage, though British rule (1815-1948) introduced Western influences.

Buddhism spread across Southeast Asia from 250 BCE, with Theravada Buddhism reaching Burma and Thailand by 500s CE. It flourished under various kingdoms until modern times, though Cambodia's Buddhist institutions were severely impacted by the Khmer Rouge (1975-1978).

Theravada Buddhism closely reflects Buddha's original teachings, with the Pali canon as its primary source. Its practitioners aim to become "arhats" (enlightened individuals). This school emphasizes monastic life and discipline, maintaining strict adherence to precepts. The path to arhatship focuses on mindfulness and meditation practices.

East Asian Buddhism : China, Korea, Japan

Buddhism spread from China to Korea and Japan, sharing common texts like the Chinese Tripitaka while developing distinct characteristics. Entering China via the Silk Road (206 BCE-220 CE), it reached Korea in the 300s and Japan in the 500s. Despite some opposition, Buddhism flourished in China during the Tang dynasty (618-907) and remained prominent until declining in the 1900s, particularly after the 1949 Communist takeover. Today, it thrives in Taiwan and Hong Kong.

The Chinese Buddhist canon (Tripitaka) evolved as monks translated Indian texts and added Chinese writings. Starting with 2,000 texts in the 500s CE, the modern version (1924-1932) contains 2,184 works across 55 books, plus 45 books of Japanese works.

1. Teaching texts (Sutras): 1,081 works

2. Rules for monks and nuns (Vinaya): 85 works

3. Philosophy and explanations (Treatises): 154 works

A fourth section contains 342 additional Indian and Chinese writings.

Chinese Buddhism combines Indian schools (Vinaya, Kosa, Madhyamaka, Yogacara, Mantrayana) with native schools (Chan, Pure Land, Tien-tai, Hua-yen), influencing Korean Son and Japanese schools like Tendai and Zen.

Buddhist schools developed different teaching methods. Early challenges with monastic rules led to Indian study trips and specialized schools. Key figures like Kumarajiva (383 CE) and Paramartha (546 CE) introduced new concepts. While Mantrayana Buddhism didn't last in China, it flourished in Japan as Shingon under Kukai (804 CE).

Ch'an Buddhism (Japanese Zen)

Zen Buddhism began in East Asia as a type of Buddhism that focuses on meditation. It was first called Ch'an in China, which means "peaceful meditation." While many people think it started with a teacher called Bodhidharma around 500 CE, meditation was already part of Chinese Buddhism before him.

In this tradition, teachers taught their wisdom directly to their students. Two important teachers, Shen-hsiu and Hui-neng, once competed to become the sixth main leader. These teachers had different views about how people become enlightened - Shen-hui thought it happened suddenly, like a light bulb turning on, while Shen-hsiu believed it happened slowly, over time. The sudden enlightenment idea eventually became more popular in Zen Buddhism.

Bodhidharma, The originator of Ch'an Buddhism taught two main ideas: that everyone has the nature of Buddha within them, and that nothing lasts forever. He believed people could suddenly understand these truths.

Ch'an Buddhism is very practical and simple. It focuses on three main things:

- Sitting quietly in meditation (called ***tso ch'an*** in Chinese or zazen in Japanese)

- Staying aware during daily activities

- Learning from a teacher

Teachers often used puzzling stories and questions (called koans) to help students think differently. Here's an example:

Question: "Isn't following Buddha's way enlightenment?"

Answer: "Having nothing is better than having something."

After some government restrictions in 842-845, two main schools of Ch'an Buddhism survived:

- Lin Chi (Rinzai): Known for using puzzling riddles to teach

- Ts'ao Tung (Soto): Focused on meditation, later led by Dogen in Japan

PS : Dogen's 'Shobogenzo' is a delight to read for any zen practitioner.

Main features of Chan (Zen) Buddhism :

1. Meditation: Chan Buddhism places a strong emphasis on meditation as the primary means of achieving enlightenment. This is reflected in the name "Chan," which is derived from the Sanskrit word "dhyana," meaning "meditation."

2. Direct experience: Chan Buddhists believe that enlightenment cannot be attained through intellectual understanding or studying scriptures. Instead, it must be experienced directly through meditation and other practices.

3. Mind-to-mind transmission: Chan Buddhism emphasizes the transmission of enlightenment from teacher to student. This is often done through direct, face-to-face encounters, such as the famous "flower sermon" in which the Buddha is said to have transmitted enlightenment to his disciple Mahakasyapa by holding up a flower.

4. Emphasis on the present moment: Chan Buddhists believe that the present moment is the only reality. They emphasize the importance of being mindful of the present moment and not dwelling on the past or worrying about the future.

5. *Use of koans:* Koans are paradoxical riddles that are used in Chan practice to help students break through their intellectual understanding and experience enlightenment.

6. *Iconoclasm:* Chan Buddhism is often iconoclastic, meaning that it rejects the use of images and symbols. This is because Chan Buddhists believe that enlightenment cannot be represented by anything that is created or conceptualized.

Tien-t'ai and Hua-yen Buddhism

Around 500 CE, many Buddhist texts from India were translated into Chinese. Two important schools of Buddhism then developed in China: Tien-t'ai and Hua-yen. They believed that Buddha taught different things to different people based on what they could understand.

The Tien-t'ai school was started by a teacher named Chih-i (538-597). He organized Buddhist teachings into simple groups and focused on an important text called the Lotus Sutra (The Threefold Truth).

His main teaching was that everything in life is temporary, empty of permanent existence, and connected to everything else. He taught both deep ideas and practical ways to meditate.

The Hua-yen school was created by Tu-shun (557-640) and later developed by Fa-tsang (643-712). They focused on another important text called the Flower Garland Sutra. Like the Tien-t'ai school, they taught that all things in the universe are connected to each other. Main features of both schools:

Tien Tai Buddhism :

Tien Tai Buddhism is based on the teachings of the Lotus Sutra & focuses on "three truths" & practise of "three samadhis". These three truths are not separate but are different aspects of the same reality.

Emptiness: All phenomena are empty of inherent existence. They do not have a separate, independent existence.

Provisional existence: Phenomena do exist, but their existence is provisional and dependent on other factors.

Middle way: The middle way is the synthesis of emptiness and provisional existence. It is the understanding that reality is both empty and existent.

Walking samadhi: This is a form of meditation in which the practitioner walks in a circle while chanting the name of the Buddha.

Sitting samadhi: This is a form of meditation in which the practitioner sits in meditation posture and focuses on the breath.

Pratibhana samadhi: This is a form of meditation in which the practitioner contemplates the nature of reality.

Hua Yen Buddhism

Hua Yen Buddhism is based on the teachings of the Avatamsaka Sutra. It emphasizes the concept of "interpenetration": & "Four Dharmadhatus".

Interpenetration: All phenomena are interconnected and interdependent. They are not separate entities but are part of a vast network of relationships.

The dharmadhatu of principle: This is the realm of ultimate reality, which is beyond all concepts and distinctions.

The dharmadhatu of phenomena: This is the realm of the phenomenal world, which is made up of all the individual things that exist.

The dharmadhatu of non-obstruction of principle and phenomena: This is the realm in which the ultimate reality and the phenomenal world are not separate but interpenetrate each other.

The dharmadhatu of interpenetration of all phenomena: This is the realm in which all phenomena are interconnected and interdependent.

Tien Tai Buddhism is more focused on the practice of meditation and the development of wisdom. Hua Yen Buddhism is more focused on the study of the scriptures and the development of understanding.

Nichiren Buddhism

Nichiren Buddhism started in Japan in the 1200s, created by a teacher named Nichiren (1222-1282). At the time, he saw problems in both Japanese Buddhism and society, so he created a simpler way to practice Buddhism.

His main teaching was very straightforward: chant a special phrase called the **daimoku.** This special chant is ***"na-mu myo-ho-ren-ge-kyo."*** It honors the Lotus Sutra, which Nichiren believed was Buddha's most important teaching.

- Nam (南): Derived from the Sanskrit "namas," meaning

"devotion" or "to dedicate one's life." It signifies dedicating oneself to the Mystic Law.

- Myoho (妙法): Translates to "Mystic Law" or "Wonderful Law." It refers to the ultimate truth or principle that permeates all existence, the interconnectedness and potential for Buddhahood inherent in all life.

- Renge (蓮華): Means "lotus flower." The lotus symbolizes purity, enlightenment, and the blossoming of potential amidst challenging circumstances. It represents the potential for Buddhahood to emerge from the mud of suffering.

- Kyo (経): Refers to a sutra or teaching.

This chant is more than recitation - it's an act of faith and self-reflection that helps practitioners connect with their Buddha nature and transform their lives. Nichiren got his ideas from two other forms of Buddhism - Tendai Buddhism and Pure Land Buddhism. He taught that simply chanting this phrase could help people improve their lives and make society better.

Nichiren was known for speaking his mind and challenging old ways of doing things. After he died, his ideas became even more popular. Today, his teachings live on through various groups in Japan, especially the Nichiren Shoshu (Soka Gakkai). This group has become involved in Japanese politics and has gained many followers in Europe and America since the 1960s.

Northern Buddhism : Tibet & Mongolia

Buddhism came to Tibet in two main periods. First, when King Srong-bsan-sgam-po married wives from Nepal and China, bringing both Indian and Chinese Buddhism to Tibet. However, Buddhism didn't become very popular right away. It grew stronger during King Khri Srong-lde-brtsan's time (756-797), when Padmasambhava and Santaraksita built Tibet's first monastery called bSam-yas.

At this monastery, an important discussion took place (792-794) about how people reach enlightenment. The Indian teachers believed it happens gradually, while Chinese teachers thought it happens suddenly. The Indian view won and became the standard in Tibet. After a time when Buddhism was banned (838-842), a teacher named Atisa (982-1054) helped bring it back. His book "Lamp on the Path to Awakening" became very important in Tibetan Buddhism.

Over the years, Tibetan Buddhists translated many texts into two main collections:

1. The Kanjur - Buddha's teachings

2. The Tenjur - explanations of these teachings

The Kanjur, made in the early 1300s, has about 700-800 texts in 100 volumes. It was first printed in Beijing in 1410 and contains seven types of teachings:

1. Rules for monks and nuns

2. Wisdom teachings

3. Flower Ornament teachings

4. Jewel Peak teachings

5. General teachings (Sutras)

6. Teachings about reaching final peace

7. Special meditation practices (Tantra)

The general teachings make up one-third of the Kanjur, meditation practices make up one-fifth, and rules for monks and nuns make up one-eighth. The Tenjur collection has over 3,500 texts about Buddhist philosophy and psychology in more than 200 volumes.

There are four main schools of Tibetan Buddhism:

1. The Nyingma School: The oldest school, started by Padmasambhava. It's known for its hidden teachings and has nine levels of learning, from basic ideas to advanced practices called Dzogchen.

2. The Kagyu School: Started by Naropa, it combines regular Buddhist teachings with special meditation. One branch, called Karma Kagyu, is famous for finding reborn teachers.

3. The Sakya School: Started in 1073, it passes down teachings through both monks and the Khon family. It was very important in Tibet from 1100-1350.

4. The Gelugpa School: Became the most powerful school in Tibet. Started by Tsongkhapa in the 1300s, it focused on monastery education and step-by-step spiritual practice. The title "Dalai Lama" was first given to a teacher named Sonam Gyatso by a Mongolian leader. The fifth Dalai Lama later became Tibet's leader in the 1600s, but it's important to know that the Dalai Lama doesn't lead all of Tibetan Buddhism - he's not like the Pope in Catholicism.

In 1950, Tibet went through a terrible time when Chinese forces took over the country. The Dalai Lama had to escape to India in 1959. After this, the Chinese military caused great harm to Tibet's Buddhist culture - they killed about one million people and destroyed more than 6,000 Buddhist temples and monasteries.

Main features of Tibetan Buddhism

Vajrayana Buddhism: Tibetan Buddhism is a form of Vajrayana Buddhism, which emphasizes the use of tantric practices to achieve enlightenment. These practices include meditation on deities, the recitation of mantras, and the visualization of mandalas.

Reincarnation: Tibetan Buddhism is known for its system of reincarnating lamas, such as the Dalai Lama. This system is based on the belief that enlightened beings can choose to be reborn in order to continue helping others.

Monasticism: Monasticism is an important part of Tibetan Buddhism. Monks and nuns play a central role in preserving and transmitting the teachings.

Deities: Tibetan Buddhism has a large pantheon of deities, who are seen as manifestations of enlightened qualities.

Rituals: Rituals are an important part of Tibetan Buddhist practice. They are used to invoke blessings, purify negative karma, and develop positive qualities.

The Tibetan wheel of existence

The Wheel of Life is an important symbol in Tibetan Buddhism that shows how life, death, and rebirth are connected. It's a circular diagram that represents important Buddhist teachings about how our actions and choices affect our lives.

*The wheel is held by Yama, the god of death. Around the outside of the wheel are 12 pictures that show how one thing leads to another in life: - A blind person (showing ignorance) - A potter making a pot (showing how we shape our future) - A monkey picking fruit (showing awareness) - A boat on water (showing our mind and body) - A house with six windows (showing our five senses plus mind) - Two people hugging (showing how we connect with things) - Someone hit by an arrow (showing feelings) - Someone drinking (showing wanting things) - Someone grabbing fruit (showing attachment) - A pregnant woman (showing how actions lead to results) - A woman giving birth (showing new life beginning) - Someone carrying a dead body (showing old age and death) Inside these pictures are six different worlds where beings can be reborn: gods at the top, then jealous gods, animals, hell beings, hungry spirits, and humans. The wheel also shows beings moving up (getting better rebirths) on the left side and down (getting worse rebirths) on the right side. At the very center of the wheel are three animals that represent the main causes of our problems: - A rooster (representing greed) - A snake (representing hatred) - A pig (representing confusion) This wheel is still used today in Tibetan Buddhism to teach people about how our actions and choices affect our future.**

Western Propagation of Buddhism

Buddhism first came to Europe in 200 BCE when a Greek official visited India. For the next 1,500 years, Europeans had little contact with Buddhist teachings. Things changed in the 1200s when Europeans like Marco Polo started traveling to Asia more often.

In the 1700s and 1800s, Europeans became more interested in Buddhism. Scholars began translating Buddhist texts, and some Europeans even started practicing Buddhism. Here are some of the first Western Buddhists:

- Madame Blavatsky and Colonel Olcott became Buddhists in Sri Lanka in 1890

- Allan Bennett became a Buddhist monk in Burma in 1901

- Anthon Gueth became a Buddhist monk in Sri Lanka

- Madame Alexandra David-Neel studied Buddhism in Tibet in 1912

Buddhism spread in Western countries in two ways: through Asian people moving to the West and through Westerners learning about Buddhism. A big change happened in 1959 when many Tibetan Buddhists had to leave Tibet and moved to India. This helped bring Eastern and Western Buddhist practices closer together.

Today, you can find these main types of Buddhism in Western countries:

- Tibetan Buddhism - found in Europe, the United States, Australia, and New Zealand

- Japanese Zen Buddhism - very popular in the United States

- The Soka Gakkai movement

- Theravada Buddhist temples and meditation centers

- New Buddhist groups started in the West, like the Western Buddhist Order (created in 1967)

While Buddhism still has relatively few followers in Western countries, more people are becoming Buddhist monks and teachers, and public interest in Buddhism continues to grow. Though Buddhism eventually faded in India, leaving only ancient ruins, it flourished elsewhere. In the 20th century, Buddhism made two important moves: it spread to the West and returned to India. Today, despite historical challenges like the violence of the Khmer Rouge and Cultural Revolution, Buddhism continues to thrive in many forms.

Sources of Potential Error in this book and Their Resolution

Before Buddhist teachings were written down, they were passed on by word of mouth. Monks (called Bhikkhus) would first hear Buddha's teachings and then share them with others. Special monks called Bhanakas had the job of memorizing these teachings perfectly. Even though there are many Buddhist texts, some teachings weren't reported correctly - Buddha himself knew about several cases where his words were misunderstood. There are five known examples of incorrect reporting, found in different Buddhist texts: the Alagaddupama Sutta, the Maha-Kamma-Vibhanga Sutta, the Kannakatthala Sutta, the Maha-Tanha-Sankhya Sutta, and the Jivaka Sutta. There were probably many more cases of teachings being reported wrongly, since monks often came to Buddha asking him to clarify what he meant. Mistakes were especially common when it came to teachings about karma and rebirth. This happened because these ideas also existed in the other religions, and monks sometimes mixed up these older beliefs with Buddha's actual teachings. So we need to be careful when reading ancient Buddhist texts and deciding if they really contain Buddha's exact words.

Fortunately, we can use three simple tests to help us:

1. Buddha was logical and reasonable in his thinking. So if something sounds logical and reasonable, it's more likely to be his actual teaching.

2. Buddha only taught things that would help people live better lives. If a teaching doesn't help people's wellbeing, it probably isn't really from Buddha.

3. Buddha was very clear about what he was certain of and what he wasn't. For things he was sure about, he gave firm answers. For things he wasn't sure about, he gave tentative answers. When we come across Buddhist teachings that seem questionable, we should use these three tests to help figure out if they truly represent Buddha's views.

Epilogue

This book has aimed to provide more than a mere accumulation of facts about Buddhism. It has sought to serve as an invitation for introspection and a deeper understanding of one's own mind. The life of the Buddha has been presented not as that of a distant historical figure, but as a relatable individual who grappled with existential questions pertinent to all.

The teachings explored are not presented as dogma, but rather as practical tools for navigating life's inherent challenges and cultivating happiness. Meditation, similarly, is not portrayed as an esoteric ritual, but as a readily accessible method for achieving inner peace and wisdom amidst the complexities of modern life. Regular meditation, regardless of duration, can contribute to genuine well-being. It is encouraged to begin a practice.

This book serves as an introduction, a signpost pointing towards a path that must be traversed individually. A true understanding of Buddhism requires experiential engagement, a process of self-examination, confronting personal fears, extending compassion to oneself and others, maintaining consistent awareness, directing thoughts and actions towards the highest good, and striving for ethical conduct.

The wisdom of the Buddha remains relevant in contemporary society. Humanity continues to experience suffering, conflict, and the pursuit of material possessions. However, the potential for inner peace and compassion exists within each individual. This capacity is not divinely bestowed, but rather an inherent aspect of human nature, awaiting cultivation.

The journey of self-discovery is not without its challenges. Doubts and periods of stagnation are inevitable. However, it is important to recall that even the Buddha encountered significant obstacles, both internal and external. His perseverance ultimately led to enlightenment. This serves as an inspiration for others to pursue their own path, however unique.

In the midst of a demanding and often overwhelming world, accessing inner wisdom can be difficult. However, it remains accessible through mindful attention. The methods discussed in this book are offered as practical tools. Self-compassion is paramount throughout this process. The pursuit of enlightenment is not a competition. It is a gradual unfolding, akin to a flower blossoming, as self-understanding and comprehension of life deepen. It is a continuous journey that begins with a single step. It is hoped that the reader will proceed with awareness, kindness, and a commitment to ongoing learning and growth, ultimately discovering their own path to peace and joy.

"There are countless beings in the world; we promise to help them all find their way.

We have many faults within ourselves; we promise to overcome them all.

There are endless truths to learn; we promise to understand them all.

The Buddha's path is the highest path; we promise to follow it completely.

Great Buddha, I put my complete trust in you, whose light shines freely in all directions.

I deeply wish to live in your peaceful land.

When I think of your realm, I see that it is greater than all others. It is as vast and endless as the sky itself.

Your kindness and caring follow the right path, coming from all the good deeds you have done.

our light reaches everywhere, just like the sun and moon.

May everyone who comes to your land share your wisdom, just as you do.

With these words I have written, I hope to meet you face to face, Buddha.

And I pray that all living beings and I may find our way to your Land of Peace and Joy."

-Excerpt from Encyclopadia of Religion & Ethics, Vol. X, p. 168-169.

* * *

Bibliography

1. Bodhi B, trans. The Middle Length Discourses of the Buddha (Majjhima Nikāya). Boston: Wisdom Publications; 2000.
2. Bodhi B, trans. The Connected Discourses of the Buddha (Samyutta Nikāya). Boston: Wisdom Publications; 2005.
3. Bodhi B, trans. The Numerical Discourses of the Buddha (Anguttara Nikāya). Boston: Wisdom Publications; 2012.
4. Bodhi B, ed. In the Buddha's Words: An Anthology of Discourses from the Pāli Canon. Boston: Wisdom Publications; 2005.
5. Bodhi B, trans. Dhammapada: The Buddha's Path of Wisdom. Berkeley: Parallax Press; 2011.
6. Bodhi B. A Comprehensive Manual of Abhidhamma: The Philosophical Psychology of Buddhism. Kandy: Buddhist Publication Society; 2000.
7. Bodhi B. The Noble Eightfold Path: Way to the End of Suffering. Kandy: Buddhist Publication Society;
8. Bodhi B. Mindfulness: A Practical Guide to Awakening.
9. Gethin R. Foundations of Buddhism. Oxford: Oxford University Press; 1998.
10. The Mahavastu ("Great Story") . J.J.Jones
11. Vaidya PL, trans. The Lalitavistara ("Graceful Description"). Darbhanga: Mithila Institute
2. Aśvaghoṣa. The Buddhacarita ("Acts of the Buddha"). Johnston EH, trans.
13. The Jātaka or Stories of the Buddha's Former Births. Cowell EB, ed.
14. Ambedkar BR. The Buddha and His Dhamma. Bombay: People's Education Society; 1957 15. Goenka SN., Vipassana Meditation.

www.ingramcontent.com/pod-product-compliance
Lightning Source LLC
LaVergne TN
LVHW091153150826
845672LV00005B/1138

* 9 7 9 8 8 9 7 2 4 7 0 4 2 *